Can a Church Live Again?

Ronny Russell

SMYTH&HELWYS
PUBLISHING, INCORPORATED · MACON, GEORGIA

Smyth & Helwys Publishing, Inc.
6316 Peake Road
Macon, Georgia 31210-3960
1-800-747-3016
©2004 by Smyth & Helwys Publishing
All rights reserved.
Printed in the United States of America.

The paper used in this publication meets the minimum
requirements of American National Standard for Information
Sciences—Permanence of Paper for Printed Library
Materials. ANSI Z39.48–1984. (alk. paper)

Library of Congress Cataloging-in-Publication Data

Russell, Ronald 1947–
        Can a church live again? the revitalization of a 21st-century church
        by Ronald Russell.
        p.   cm.

        1. Church renewal.
        2. Mission Baptist Church (Locust, N.C.)
        I. Title.
        BV600.3 .R77   2003
        286'.175673—dc22

                                                            2003020685
                                                            CIP
ISBN 1-57312-418-4 (pbk.)

Inclusion of various websites does not indicate personal endorsement.

Contents

Acknowledgements

A story that covers more than a decade involves a lot of people to whom much gratitude and acknowledgement must be given. The beginning place is easy. It has to begin with my dear wife of thirtyfive years, a "reluctant warrior" who has endured the stresses and celebrated the victories with me. In many years the stresses far outweighed the victories. She didn't sign up in the beginning to be a pastor's wife and I'm sure there were days, if not years, when she must have wished I would just leave well enough alone. She is elated with the church that has emerged and especially so because children and others deemed "the least of these" can find at Mission a place where they can find grace and feel at home.

There are numerous staff people to acknowledge; people who must have wished often that I would have been less "visionary" and more attentive to details and practicality. Kolis Moore and Koni Huneycutt, music ministers extraordinaire, along with their dad Hoyle Whitley who preceded them, added to the creative mix during years when we all wondered if we would have enough energy remaining for the next Sunday. We have been partners in ministry for over twenty years and they have never stopped being supportive, encouraging, and patient.

Two administrative assistants have been more than employees. Bonnie Preslar and Brenda Bost before her, not only worked like Troians but also fueled the fires of transition with their sense of humor, professional demeanor, and creativity. Darrell Williams has come on board in an associate role in the last four years to give help and to partner with us in the dream.

Eddie Hammett, mentioned several times in the book, has been a constant source of inspiration and encouragement. His creative genius for understanding how the church must work for a new day, has fueled my own inspiration. His inexhaustible encouragement and support have helped me through many a lonely and dark period. No "dark night of the soul" is ever really hopeless with people like Eddie to shine the light along the path.

I wish I could name all the people of the congregation at Mission Baptist Church. They were not only tolerant of my sometimes radical and rebellious ways, but more often than not, they gave their blessing to birthing something new, even when they didn't always understand where we were going or know what the outcome would be. To avoid the risk of leaving out someone really important, I must acknowledge a handful of unnamed people who have been fiercely loyal friends, revolutionaries at times, consummate disciple-makers, and some of the most mature Christians I have ever known. They know who they arc they are the ones who send the notes, the e-mails, and make the phone calls at just the right time. They are the ones with whom I've traveled to conferences, talked to hours on end, prayed with, wept with, and rejoiced with through these years of exciting and sometimes frightening ministry. Sharlina Honeycutt, the quintessential English teacher, deserves special acknowledgement for proofreading.

Finally, I must dedicate this writing to a dear saint of God who just this year went to be with her dear Jesus: Opal Whitley. She was my prayer warrior, my note writer, my telephone caller, my greatest source of encouragement, year after year. She didn't always understand all that we were trying to accomplish but she never wavered in her support and encouragement. I shall never forget her.

Ronny Russell
2003

Foreword

Can a Church Live Again? is an opportunity to walk with a pastor and a 100-year-old congregation through a journey from complacency and routine to intentionality, challenge, and growth. When I first met Ronny Russell, he was facing burnout, despair, and deep feelings of aimlessness. He had been pastor of Mission Baptist Church for more than fifteen years and felt he was stuck in a routine of pastoral care and institutional maintenance. He found little personal or professional fulfillment in such a routine. His rural congregation seemed also to be plateaued in their ministry. Ronny knew there should be more to ministry than this, but he needed help finding his way back to the roots of his call to ministry and the biblical mission of the church.

You will find great hope, encouragement, guidance, and proven principles on each page as the author shares personal stories from his journey and those of his congregation and community. The power of the faith stories is incredible and true. Certainly, transformed leaders transform churches and communities. Because Mission Baptist Church has become intentional over the last twelve years in becoming a disciple-making congregation, they have recaptured the joy of ministry. God has so blessed their efforts that they have some who drive 30-plus miles to participate in church and small group ministries. They've gone from one struggling worship service to two thriving services looking at the prospects of a third service. They've helped the hurting, those in personal, professional, and spiritual crises.

You will read stories of laypeople who are so excited and equipped for ministry that they beat the pastor and staff to the side of the hospitalized and people in need. You will hear of a congregation who thinks more of how to reach those on the outside of the church walls than keeping themselves comfortable on the inside of the church walls.

You will learn how a pastor reclaimed his calling, discerned his unique equipping ministry, and discovered anew the joy and fulfillment of ministry. Ronny allows you to see his struggles and his successes. He has learned much through the school of hard knocks, and now he shares them in hopes that it might help soften the life lessons of your journey of personal, spiritual, and professional renewal.

How blessed I have been, and I think you will be, by walking through this journey of spiritual and organizational renewal. Yes, an established comfortable church can change—if it really wants to. The journey is tough but worth it in light of the Kingdom's calling and the biblical mandates our Lord has set for his church.

If you're struggling with despair or feelings of inadequacy about your leadership and your church, this book is for you. You will learn of Holy Discontentment, the Stirring of Waters, Principles of Change and Transitioning, The Role of the Outside Prophet, and How to Count the Cost. You and your leaders will also learn valuable proven lessons of leadership in moving a church from maintenance to mission, from comfort to challenge, and you will have the opportunity to dream new dreams, explore new questions and adventures of laypeople in leadership, read about laypeople seeking God's ministry for them and pastors and staff who seek to learn how to make disciples through their equipping ministries. What a wonderful journey it is. I can't wait to see what God does in the next chapter of this congregation's life and the life of their lay and pastoral leaders. Keep up with their new adventures by visiting www.missionchurch.org or www.transformingsolutions.org

Edward H. Hammett
Author of Making the Church Work, The Gathered and Scattered Church, *and* Reframing Spiritual Formation

Introduction: The Journey

What's it like to turn a church around? We hear that question often at Mission Baptist Church, the North Carolina church that I pastor, these days. Indeed, what's it like? One volume alone cannot communicate the work, the pain, the joy, the frustration, and the rewards of such an endeavor. Let me add that we, the congregation and myself, have only begun to turn the church around. Our destination is still off in the distance, and we never expect to reach it fully.

However, we have made giant strides. In the Old Testament book of Job, the most unfortunate central character suffered all the loss and grief one man could handle. His plight was so devastating that he lamented his day of birth. Job's friends were no help, actually adding to his misery. His wife even encouraged him to curse God and die.

Finally, Job began to question his existence. Why was he here? If he went the way of all people—to death—what would happen next? Job asked the question of the ages: *If mortals die, can they live again? This thought would give me hope, and through my struggle I would eagerly wait for release* (14:14, NLT).

Churches throughout North America are dying. In fact, some are dead and buried, while others barely survive on life support. Then there are those, alive and struggling, that show discernable signs of decline and demise. Mission Baptist Church showed these signs fifteen years ago.

We live in exciting but critical times for the church. Many churches are perfectly content to be headed in the wrong direction. Others want to turn around but lack the motivation or courage to take the necessary steps.

Which leads to the Job-like question, can a church live again? If we believe God constantly renews and restores, we must answer yes without hesitation. A church can live again if empowered by the Holy Spirit. Still, new life does not come without struggle. This book is an attempt to offer churches Job's hope that God can bring the dead or dying to life. I pray that numerous pastors, staff, and churches will read this book and find hope for their situations.

Holy Discontent

Miz Louisa, she believe in God with all her soul. But she don't subscribe to church much. She say the way some folk run they's churches, it take God right out cha heart.[1]

In the 1970s and 1980s, a handful of men roughly organized as a "men's group" met at Mission Baptist Church. They existed as a missions organization, which only meant that when they met, they briefly discussed subjects relating to missions. The women's group, on the other hand, was more "directly" involved in missions, praying at every monthly meeting for missionaries on their birthdays. For years, the men's group was little more than a "meet and eat" crowd. Leader after leader attempted in vain to revive the group, offering "more interesting" programs, better food, or better meeting times. These attempts at renewal never worked for long. The men's group became one of those typical church programs that never seem to flourish and yet never seem to die.

That is to say, this was the case before Mission Baptist Church became a "disciple-making church." By 1998, the once-floundering organization called the Baptist Men had redefined their purpose. Enlisting several women on their team, they became the Missions Emphasis Team (M.E.T.). Their purpose was to organize mission projects, raise awareness in the church body concerning missions, and join with any other body of believers or denomination to carry out the Great Commission.

By spring 1999, ten of them had committed to going to Honduras for a mission trip. Most of the men were growing disciples, and many belonged to one of the small accountability groups that had sprung up in the church. This mission trip to Honduras would have a profound effect on the life of the church. It was one of those signal events that took the church to the next level in terms of our commitment to making disciples.

Other trips were planned immediately upon their return. In 1999, floods that accompanied Hurricane Floyd devastated many communities in eastern North Carolina. Buoyed by the success and inspiration of their Honduras trip, the missions group raised the consciousness of the entire church to undertake a flood recovery mission project. Thirty-three responded and traveled to the eastern part of the state in 2000 for up to a week.

The group held a barbecue chicken dinner to raise funds for the project. T-shirts bearing the church name were printed and handed out for the project's participants. They gave me one as an "honorary" member of the group, even though I did not plan to go on the trip. Later that day, I took a closer look at the back of the shirt. It read, "Building Disciples." These two words spoke volumes to me about how far our church had come. I realized we had finally moved from a program-based church to a ministry-based church, from maintenance to mission. People were beginning to understand the difference. By 2002, forty-five different people (about 15 percent of regular Sunday morning attendees) were involved in short-term mission trips to places like Mexico, Brazil, Honduras, West Virginia, and Alaska.

You Have Come to the Right Place

Other incidents also signaled our transformation. Delores was in her early twenties when she first attended our church. At a family reunion, her aunt and uncle—Barry and Darlene—invited her to visit Mission Baptist. Newly married, Delores could not persuade her husband to come, and so she came alone. Her spiritual hunger was evident. One Sunday morning, she presented herself for church membership after making a profession of faith. By then I knew more about her and knew how difficult it would be for a twenty-two-year-old wife to undertake her spiritual journey without the support of her husband.

I remember thinking, *Delores, you have come to the right place. Here, we will disciple you. Here, we will take care of you and nurture you in your*

Christian faith. I was somewhat taken aback by my own thoughts. Why did I think that about our church? Because it was true. Delores would have had a tough time fitting in at most churches, and although I knew it would not be easy at our church, I also knew that the infrastructure was in place to help her grow and be nurtured. More than that, I knew our people's hearts, which had been set ablaze by the spirit of God. They were growing in oneness with God and in their desire to become disciples of Jesus.

Within a few weeks, Delores had joined a small group. Because of her work schedule, she found little time to attend at first. The group was patient with her. Delores had recently begun a hair-styling business and took appointments whenever people wanted them. She shared her financial struggles with the group. The next week, Mike, one of the group members, called Delores and asked for a haircut appointment. Mike and his wife Sally and other members of the group reached out to Delores in a number of ways over the next several months. When Delores became pregnant, they organized a baby shower involving the small group and other people in the church.

How did I know our people would take care of Delores? There was no guarantee, of course, but I had seen it happen before, and I knew that compassion and care are always present where disciples are being made.

Where Disciples Are Being Made

One day as I prepared for my lunch break, a young man appeared at the office door. He asked if he could talk with me for a few minutes. When he sat down, he began to pour out the story of his sordid past. Only twenty-three years old, he had been released from prison the day before. He wanted to share his prison conversion. He also desired help in his faith journey. In essence, he was looking for someone to disciple him. As with Delores, I remember thinking to myself, *Young man, you have come to the right place.* What gave me that assurance? Acceptance and opportunities for spiritual growth are always present where disciples are being made.

Though this young man has taken several steps backward since his conversion, I am not disappointed in him. Two older men in the church took him under their wings. Even when he repeatedly let them down, they never gave up on him. Another businessman in the church gave him a job. Josh continues to struggle and probably will for a long time. Yet people believe in him and will not give up on him. This kind of support happens in a church whose people are growing disciples of Jesus Christ.

The Last One Called

Julie was a prayer coordinator for one of our adult Bible fellowships (ABF), or Sunday school classes. One night, she called to tell me about the death of her ABF classmate's grandfather. Perhaps the most significant thing about her phone call was that I was not the first person Julie called that night. She had already activated the prayer chain in her ABF and notified Gary's small group leader. Later, I would learn that almost the entire small group and several of Gary's ABF classmates went to the funeral home during the visitation. When Gary came back to the small group after the funeral, he expressed what the group's ministry had meant to him.

A Major Paradigm Shift

Another indication of a change in our church was that the senior pastor was no longer considered the "first responder" in a crisis. The fact that I was called at all was not even a common occurrence. Julie simply said, "I thought you might like to know." The call seemed like an afterthought, made after the *real* ministers had been called. In a disciple-making church, all members are ministers. Everyone understands this and everyone affirms it. It is as natural as breathing. As Robert Slocum stated in his book *Maximize Your Ministry*, "The early church had a commissioning service for lay ministry; it was called baptism."[2]

Stories like Julie's happen almost weekly, sometimes several times a week. Linda, a young wife and mother, was rushed to the hospital one night for emergency surgery. Her small group leader, Danny, called me with the news. I learned that before he called me, he activated the ABF prayer chain, and Linda's small group swung into action. Danny went to the hospital and prayed with Linda before surgery. They wanted me to know so I could pray for Linda too, but my presence wasn't expected at all. The real ministers were present and active, and that was enough.

Heavily Programmed

Before the turnaround, Mission Baptist was a typical Southern Baptist church. We were heavily programmed, offering Sunday school, Women's Missionary Union, Royal Ambassadors for boys, Girls in Action for girls, Acteens for teenage girls, January Bible Study, Christmas programs, summer camps, etc.

Then, of course, there was the blessed Sunday night worship service. Some members perceived this service as the real test of the faithful. If they could somehow endure another hour of special music and preaching, then surely they must have special place in heaven. A mere fraction of Sunday morning attendees came back to worship on Sunday nights. Personally, I have concluded that Sunday evening worship is one of the single greatest deterrents to making disciples in churches that still insist on having them. First of all, it is another hour of programming people feel obligated to attend. Secondly, those who attend feel they have done their religious duty, and therefore there is no need for further Bible study, fellowship, or ministry. Certainly, the Sunday evening service fills a need for some people. However, it is usually a fellowship need that can be met in countless other ways that are more productive and require less of the church's resources and energy. Some cutting-edge churches use Sunday evenings to provide a time of worship with a different style for those who cannot or will not come on Sunday morning.

We never had a strong Wednesday night service. To be like our neighbors, we tried prayer meetings from time to time. These lasted for a couple of years until I pulled the plug on the ill-fated endeavor. Our last prayer meeting took place in the mid-1980s. The handful was unusually small that night—eight of us, to be exact. Four of them were my wife, my teenaged daughter, my elementary school-aged son, and I. I decided not to hold the meeting again unless someone asked about it. The following week, I didn't put it in the bulletin. To this day, some fifteen years later, no one has ever asked what happened to Wednesday night prayer meeting.

According to Scripture, when Jesus stood on the Mount of Olives and looked over the vast city of Jerusalem, he wept because they had gotten so far off track (Luke 19:41-42). In contrast, we look at our cities, towns, and country villages and say, "Hmmm, let's see. Which of our programs will work for this problem?"

A Generation Lost

In the early nineties, I read a book by George Barna titled *The Frog in the Kettle*. Looking out over the threshold of the 1990s, Barna made a bold prediction that unless the church radically reformed, they would lose a whole generation of people. He felt that the church had one more chance to reach the Boomers (those born between 1946 and 1964), and if we did not become relevant to them, they would never give the church another chance.

Barna was prophetic. There was a surge of attendance in the early 1990s. Then the surge subsided. By the middle of the decade, church attendance had hit an all-time low in the United States. The church failed to reach the Boomers. They came for a while to bring their children, but as their children grew up, the Boomers dropped out because nothing was done to retain them by meeting their needs. I believe that if/when they returned to church, they remembered why they had originally stopped coming: boredom, staid traditions, and irrelevance. These elements drove them away both in their early years and then later in their thirties and forties.

Their spiritual hunger had not gone away, however. I talked with people who had remained in our congregation in the early 1990s and discovered that many of them were as restless and discontent as I was. The question was often framed in terms of "Is this all there is to church?" If people inside the church asked these questions, what questions did those outside the church ask? More tragically, had non-churchgoers stopped asking questions out of apathy?

Holy Handyman

I came out of seminary in 1975 full of idealism about how we could change the world. In late 1974, the people of Mission Baptist Church called me as their first full-time pastor in nearly two decades. I knew little about the institutional church. Seminary sparked a vision and a hunger to elevate the church to new heights of social and evangelistic fervor, but there was little practical training about how to do this.

Within a few years, I was unwittingly consumed by the institution. I took on the role that was expected of me. I became the village priest. One matriarch liked to boast about how I was everybody's pastor in the community. To her, this was a good thing. To me, it was a prescription for burnout.

In 1990, I began writing in a journal, which proved therapeutic during melancholy times. One day I considered my role.

Pastor. Preacher. Clergyman. Man of the Cloth. Man of God. Shepherd. Reverend. Right Reverend. Left Reverend. Holy Man. Handy Man. Unhandy Man.

Administrator. Counselor. Exhorter. Proclaimer of the Gospel. Worship Facilitator. Comforter. Teacher. Servant. Sometimes even Janitor. C.E.O. (Chief Exhortation Officer).

What's in a name anyway? I worked like a man possessed to earn a doctor's degree. Dr. Ronny Russell. I liked the sound of it. But it never changed a thing about me. My wife still asked me to take out the garbage. Parishioners still called me to see that I got the church van serviced and gassed.

A table needs moving from one building to another. A john has overflowed— it's Monday morning and the floor is ankle deep in water. Someone's kid gets beaten up by the church bully. It's the middle of the night and a drunken husband is on the rampage. The local PTA needs a fund raiser. A marginal church member's third cousin twice removed is in the hospital.

Who you gonna call?

It's a job for…HOLY HANDYMAN.

"(He) was a caretaker in the house of God. He was responsible for the replacement of burnt-out light bulbs, and for the cleanliness of the church, and the care of the Bibles, and the hymnbooks, and the placards on the walls. On Friday night he conducted the Young Ministers' Service and preached with them. Rarely did he bring the message on a Sunday morning; only if there was no one else to speak was his father called upon. He was a kind of…holy handyman." [3]

"That's what I am," I thought. HOLY HANDYMAN.

There is no dignity in a title. Respect has to be earned. But it will never be unanimous. They even shoot at kings and presidents. They crucified Christ as a common criminal. Dignity is a measure of self-worth.

*The scriptures say it best: "Be very careful when all men speak well of you."
HOLY HANDYMAN. No one else may full understand, but I like it. It fits.*

*Preachers are noted for their mobility. They move around a lot. Sometimes of
their own volition, but more often not. Had a preacher friend once who joked that
he was having wheels installed on all his furniture. For some, it's not a joke.*

Preachers have become to some like everything else in society.

Disposable. Like a soiled diaper.

*As part of my doctoral research project, I did a survey in my church to deter-
mine attitudes toward worship. One of the questions was, "What would you change
about our present worship services?" One yokel answered, "The preacher." He/she
didn't stop there, but went on to say that preachers are like kids' Christmas toys. The
kids tire of them after a while and clamor for new ones. The new wears off. Time
for a shiny new model with fresh batteries. If the old doll walks and talks, the new
one must sweat and salivate.*

*I have no idea who wrote that answer but I am sure of one thing. He or she is
not alone in their thinking. But I wonder if he or she had any idea how much that
hurt.*

"What should I call you, Preacher?"

"Reverend? Preacher? Doctor? By your first name?"

*Some church members, older ones especially, will never be comfortable with a
first name. They respect the office too much. First name is too familiar for a holy
man. To others it doesn't matter. They want familiarity. It removes any qualms
about kicking aside the used toy.*

*Detachment. Respect. Familiarity. The ideal is somewhere in there. What's in
a title? Nothing really. People want something with which they can be
comfortable.*

Let others call me what they will. I like HOLY HANDYMAN. It fits.

Slow Burnout

I didn't crash and burn all at once. It was a gradual thing. The church
grew, and so did my workload. I was like a farmer who keeps adding more
acreage each year without hiring more help. There is only so much one
person can do. I was consumed with hospital visits, funerals, committee
meetings, home visits, administration, counseling, late-night phone calls,
and early morning breakfast meetings.

While doing these daily tasks, I was expected to prepare not one but
two dynamic sermons each week and a Bible study for Wednesday night.

The 1980s are a blur for me. I neglected my wife and children and failed to visit my aging parents nearly as much as I wanted or needed to.

I was consumed by this unrealistic (and unbiblical) role expectation. When I looked around me, however, I discovered I was not alone. Other pastors had the same pressure. One told me that when he went to bed at night, he laid out his suit and tie beside the bed in case he got a call to go to the hospital. Being on call this way on a 24/7 basis all year round cannot be a healthy way to live. I would go to a ministers' meeting and come away close to clinical depression. I experienced cynicism that I knew was unhealthy and wrong.

I drank too much coffee, ate too much fast food on the run, and consumed too many tobacco products. These were all artificial stimulants. I knew that, but I had little time for exercising the spiritual disciplines of prayer, meditation, solitude, or reflection, let alone physical exercise. On October 15, 1993, it caught up with me. I was rushed to the hospital with chest pains and diagnosed with a myocardial infarction, more commonly known as a heart attack.

Lying in a hospital's intensive care unit at age forty-six is definitely an attention-getter. However, my winter of discontent had already begun. The heart attack episode would provide the final catalyst, but the wheels had already begun turning. I was discovering that I was not alone in my "holy discontent."

Not at Home in Midian

The central event of the Old Testament is the exodus, God's delivery of his people from the bondage of slavery in Egypt. In Exodus 2 we find Moses in the backside of the desert. His employer and father-in-law Jethro was kind and generous beyond expectations. Not only did he provide employment and sustenance for Moses, but he also provided a wife in the person of his daughter Zipporah. Zipporah and Moses had a son and named him Gershom, which apparently means "I have become an alien in a strange land." Moses never felt at home in Midian. He realized from day one that he was in the wrong place.

I believe Moses' holy discontent enabled him to be more open to the burning bush experience. Meanwhile, his fellow Israelites experienced a holy discontent of their own. Back in Egypt, their bondage became more oppressive and unbearable by the day. They were desperate enough to pray, to cry out to God in their discontent.

God heard their prayers and remembered where the people had been left. God remembered the covenant with Abraham, which involved a land of promise. What were the Israelites doing in Egypt? Like Moses, they were in the wrong place and they needed a deliverer. God would use Moses for that daunting task.

Being in the wrong place on the back side of a desert was an appropriate metaphor for me as I entered midlife. I hadn't signed up to be the professional clergyperson hired to do all the ministry. I was never called to tend sheep in Midian. It became my role by default. I'm glad God remembered where I had been left.

Smoldering Tumbleweeds

If I had a burning bush experience, it was not as dramatic as that of Moses. Mine was more in the form of a few smoldering tumbleweeds. It was a process over time. God had told Abraham, "Get thee unto a land that I will show thee" (Gen 12:1 KJV). This was the covenant God renewed with Moses. In essence, Moses discovered that he was in the wrong place. The Israelites back in Egypt were coming to the same realization.

This holy discontent with one's present circumstances is a common biblical theme. It seems that God forever has to deliver his people from wrong places. Elijah experienced it before and after his battle with the prophets of Baal on Mt. Carmel. He knew there was something wrong in the land. The people wandered far from their purpose. Ahab and Jezebel led the people about as far away from God as they could get. God used Elijah to overturn the fortunes of the false prophets, but Elijah was only one person. He apparently didn't have much of a following and expressed this discontent to God: "I, even I only, am left" (1 Kgs 19:10 KJV). When he expressed his dissatisfaction with his presence circumstances, it didn't seem much like holy discontent. It seemed more like whining. However, God took the complaining and turned it into something positive for Elijah.

Sometimes we get to our Midian through actions of our own, and sometimes we are victims of circumstance. I never intended to wander from my calling. I drifted to the backside of the desert.

Fresh out of seminary and armed with a healthy balance of evangelistic fervor and social justice, I saw the church as God's catalyst to change society's ills. Save the souls and equip those souls for ministry and turn them loose on an increasingly corrupt world was the ideal planted in my soul by people like Gordon and Mary Cosby, Findley Edge, and even Billy Graham.

Somewhere along the way, I started to follow the wrong model. Instead of following Jesus, I followed the cultural model of church. This involved spending hours in hospital visitation, hours and hours preparing for three services per week, and little time left for anything else like saving the world. HOLY HANDYMAN.

It gnawed at me. Hadn't Jesus said, "Go into the world and make disciples"? The only world I was going into was a small, institutionalized world of pastoral care and preaching. I wasn't even thinking about making disciples, opting instead for programs of Sunday school and preaching and discipleship training to do whatever they could to raise the level of knowledge about God and Jesus.

My holy discontent turned into a burning bush when I began to have conversations with other people in the church who also groaned under the bondage of the wrong model for doing church. I began to hear things like "All I do is come to church three times a week and listen to somebody preach to me." "I'm tired of hearing people complain about being overworked on all these committees, and I'm tired too. Isn't there something we could do to make a difference in the world?"

Why Would Anyone Want to Join This Church?

I used to visit people in their homes and hear them say, "Preacher, our family wants to join your church." I would smile and say, "Why, that's wonderful. We would love to have you. You would be such a fine asset to our church. What would you like to do in the kingdom of God—sing in the choir or serve on the fellowship building committee?" I would leave these conversations wondering why anyone would actually want to join our church—or any church for that matter.

A book by Robert Slocum titled *Maximum Your Ministry* became essential to me in those early years of discontent. In that book, Slocum posed a pointed question, a question that still haunts me. He asked, "Once we get someone into church, then what?" I did not have a good answer to that question.

My winter of discontent was about to become my spring of hope.

An Unlikely Theophany—But Aren't They All?

Looking back, I don't know how I was able to persuade seven deacons to give up their Friday and Saturday nights to attend a deacon conference at our denomination's retreat center near Asheboro, North Carolina. Caraway Conference Center is rustic in its setting but has a hotel-type atmosphere *sans* room television and telephone.

The deacon conference is an annual event organized by our state convention personnel. It's designed to inform deacons that what they are doing is probably not biblical, and they need to provide more "spiritual" leadership to the church. I was not particularly excited about attending the conference, but several deacons had expressed an interest so I arranged for us to go. This was in 1989.

When we got there, we were swept into the usual format for conferences: a plenary session where everybody heard a keynote speaker followed by breakout sessions where conferees could choose from a variety of topics. Our group of eight (including myself) fanned out to several of the breakouts. The idea was that we would go to as many different ones as possible and then compare notes.

By the end of the Friday night session, several of the deacons had attended one particular breakout that they recommended to the rest of us. Apparently, the speaker had struck a chord with fellow malcontents. On Saturday morning, I wandered into the conference of a man named Eddie Hammett.

I have to admit I didn't have a great attitude at this conference. I had given up prime family time, and quite frankly, I was simply going through the motions. I remember purposely taking a seat in the back of the small room where perhaps twenty-five or thirty other conferees gathered. My purpose in taking a back seat was so I could lean my head against the wall and relax if the speaker failed to pique my interest.

Within five minutes, Eddie Hammett had me hooked. I cannot recall his specific words, but the gist of his remarks drove straight to my heart. Here was a young man verbalizing what many of us had felt for some time—discontent with the old model for doing church, disdain for church programs that did little to change lives, and dislike for staying on the same path we had traveled for too many years.

Later, Eddie and I had many conversations and became great friends. He wrote a couple of books and numerous articles that dealt with church reform and renewal. We also enlisted Eddie to come and lead two annual leadership retreats at our church in 1990 and 1991.

> *Come gather round people wherever you roam,*
> *And admit that the waters around you have grown,*
> *And accept it that soon you'll be drenched to the bone.*
> *If your time to you is worth saving,*
> *Then you'd better start swimming or you'll sink like a stone*
> *For the times they are a-changin'.*
>
> —Bob Dylan

Notes

1 David Baldacci, *Wish You Well* (New York: Warner Books, 2000), 231.
2 Robert Slocum, *Maximize Your Ministry* (Colorado Springs CO: NavPress, 1990), 257.
3 James Baldwin, *Go Tell It On the Mountain* (New York: Dell Books, 1965), 50-51.

Holy Discoveries

A group of senior citizens sat a dinner table in a Panama City Beach retirement community, discussing their woes.

"My arms are so weak I can hardly lift this cup of coffee," said one.

"Yes, I know. My cataracts are so bad I can't even see my coffee," said another.

"I can't turn my head because of the arthritis in my neck," said a third, to which several nodded in agreement.

"My blood pressure pills make me dizzy," another went on.

"I guess that's the price we pay for getting old," winced an old man as he slowly shook his head.

Then there was a short moment of silence, broken by one woman who said cheerfully, "Thank God we can all still drive."

Sadly and frighteningly, that humorous story is a parable for the modern church. We have deep-seeded maladies and dysfunctions, but "thank God we can still do church."

The children of Israel were deeply mired in the institution of slavery in Egypt. Through a series of miracles they were freed to pursue a life of freedom. But first they had to cross a desert and overcome their own maladies and dysfunctions. Along the way of their exodus journey, they made interesting discoveries, which can be summed up as follows:

• They discovered they had a problem. They had been in slavery for four hundred years and the enslavement was becoming more and more oppressive.

- They discovered that God had not forgotten them. God heard their cries for deliverance.
- They discovered that God would raise up the leadership they needed.
- They discovered that God was powerful enough to break the bonds of slavery.
- They discovered that God would provide for them even in the desert.
- They discovered that God could even overcome their murmurings.

Heaven, We Have a Problem!

I read in a denominational publication that on November 15, 2000, the Baptist General Association of Virginia approved a $15 million budget. Included in the budget was a new initiative called "church planting and revitalization." Almost $1.3 million was allocated for this new program. At the same time, Virginia Baptists made a 2 percent reduction in their overall budget allocations for national and worldwide ministries.

Why is this news significant? It is highly significant, I think, because a large denominational body has recognized the stagnation of its churches and has moved to do something about it. They have recognized the gravity of the problem of declining churches.

Some church bodies have called it revitalization, as in the case with Virginia Baptists. Others have called it revisioning. The old term is church renewal. The Baptist State Convention of North Carolina has recently launched a bold, new initiative called Pursuing Vital Ministry (PVM). Their aim is to help churches that are plateaued or declining to become vital again. For many, this will not mean significant growth in numbers. A lot of churches exist in regions where there is little or no population growth. For them, vital ministry may mean growth of another kind. The goal of PVM for North Carolina Baptists is to help churches become vital again. Whatever the name of the renewal process, it is important for a church to first discover and recognize that it has a problem.

After 400 years, Israel had grown tired of her enslavement. She had become spiritually stagnated and lacking in power—economically, socially, mentally, and spiritually. In her frustration, she cried out to God in prayer.

In *My Utmost for His Highest,* Oswald Chambers wrote, "If there is stagnation spiritually, never allow it to go on, but get into God's presence and find out the reason for it."[1] Spiritual stagnation can creep into an individual's life, or it can grip an entire church body.

It is fair to say that spiritual stagnation had affected not only my personal relationship with God, but it had permeated the life of Mission Baptist Church. Several things would arise to shake us out of our doldrums, but first we had to recognize the root of the problem.

What is the most common cause of the problem of spiritual stagnation? Too many churches and church leaders see the problem in the context of a cultural war. They see the culture as the culprit and blame everything from the media to rock music for the stagnated condition of the church. In response, they engage in a kind of guerilla warfare, taking shots at the culture from time to time. However, as Robert Parham wrote, "If religion is to right the ship of culture, then it must do more than cry crisis. It must appeal to human moral goodness without casting overboard the awareness of profound moral evil."[2]

Where there is a lack of vitality in the church, the root cause is most likely to be found within. I believe the church cannot impact culture until it changes itself. Too often we come across as angry and mean-spirited when we boycott theme parks and bash selected groups of sinners. We must remember Parham's words: "You can be the church in a world you wish you had, or your faith can face the world the way it really is."[3]

Gone But Not Forgotten

Israel prayed for 400 years. Moses languished for forty years tending his father-in-law's herds. Then God heard the cries of God's people and appeared to Moses.

Why did it take so long?

I am what denominational execs like to call a "long-tenured pastor," having been at my church for twenty-eight years. I never intended to stay this long. I've interviewed with a good number of pastor search committees over the years. Some of them I didn't feel would be a good fit; some of them didn't feel I was a good fit for their parish.

After we were well into our process of turning the church around, I would assess other suitor churches based on where they were in comparison to Mission. Most of them were far behind Mission in terms of moving from a traditional, program-based church to a contemporary, ministry-based church. Transitioning takes an enormous amount of energy. I agree with one church consultant who said a pastor only has one transitioning in his or her career. The toll in terms of energy spent and stress endured is just too great to do more than once for most people.

In June 2001 I attended a conference in Atlanta led by Tom Bandy, author of several books including *Coaching Change: Breaking Down Resistance, Building Up Hope.* At the conference Bandy said that all transitional pastors have had a brush with mental health problems, nervous breakdowns, physical problems, and the like. I was processing the morning session over lunch with David Hughes, pastor of the First Baptist Church in Winston-Salem, North Carolina. He, like all of us at the conference, was a bit shell-shocked by Bandy's presentation. Prophets usually leave their audiences in a state of shock. David made reference to Bandy's statement about the toll exacted on transitioning pastors. He understood precisely what Bandy was talking about, for David was in the throes of turning around a big and cumbersome train—a large, downtown, traditional First Church. It was no comfort to him at all when I pointed out to him that I had already had my heart attack. Later in the year, I talked to David again. It was in January, and he described for a group of us how utterly drained of energy he had been after coming through the Christmas season. Added to the usual stress of leading a church during Christmas was the energy he was giving in helping the church transition.

If a pastor is to be serious about transitioning a church, he/she had better be prepared to stay in it for the long haul. Moving around every few years won't work. However, after pastors have been in one place so long, they begin to wonder if God has forgotten them. On more than one Monday morning, I wondered if my file had fallen behind a filing cabinet somewhere in God's heavenly office.

I do not suggest for a moment that it takes a twenty-eight-year stint at one place before a pastor can build the trust necessary to lead a church into renewal. Rick Hughes didn't take nearly that long. Rick pastored Cartledge Creek Baptist Church near Rockingham, North Carolina, for ten years (1990–2000). The Cartledge Creek story is amazing. The church has a deep and storied history. It was organized in 1774. During Rick's tenure there, the church moved from an inward focus to an outward focus. The Sunday school, for example, transitioned from a Sunday morning program to Bible learning communities that also became ministry teams. The emphasis in Sunday school was on making disciples (what a radical idea!), and these Bible study classes became the setting where disciples could live out the core values of the Christian faith.

Rick also led the church to become involved in a small group ministry. They too placed a heavy emphasis on ministry involvement in the community. One such ministry was an outreach to a tri-county group home for special education. Another group took on a ministry to pregnant mothers referred to them by the local Department of Social Services. The church also became known for its ministry in the area of foster parenting.

Attendance quadrupled in these ten years, the budget tripled, and the worship style transitioned to a less formal and more contemporary style. In Rick's words, the most important change was that people's lives were transformed. Many of the people who experienced this life change were people who would not fit into most churches in the area. How did this happen? It happened because the church adopted a vision of making disciples and steered away from a heavy emphasis on programs and maintenance of the institution.

The point is that God will hear our cries when we are ready. He will hear our cries when we are sufficiently dissatisfied with the present situation. We don't have to move from place to place to find the quick fix to our stagnation. The following words from Eugene Peterson are to this point:

> Pastors, faced with the failure of purchased procedures (packaged programs), typically blame the congregation and leave it for another. The devil, who is behind all this smiling and lacquered mischief, so easily makes us discontent with what we are doing that we throw up our hands in the middle of it, disgusted, and go on to another parish that will appreciate our gifts in ministry and our devotion to the Lord. Every time a pastor abandons one congregation for another out of boredom or anger or restlessness, the pastoral vocation of all of us is vitiated.[4]

The Bible is filled with stories of how God always seemed to raise up the leadership needed for a crisis. In the exodus from Egypt story, Moses was the man of the hour. God found Moses on the backside of the desert. He wasn't in church. He was a shepherd, not a priest or prophet. Well, actually he was. He just didn't know it yet.

The Outside Prophet

This is he who was spoken of through the prophet Isaiah: "A voice of one calling in the desert, 'Prepare the way for the Lord, make straight paths for him.'" (Matt 3:3 NIV)

The role of the outside prophet as one to "stir the waters" of church life is such an important role that I have devoted an entire chapter to it (see chapter 6). Suffice it to say here that an outside person can lead a church to discover something about itself that no one else can do. It is no accident that much of the Old Testament is devoted to the writings of prophets. The prophets helped ancient Israel discover something important about herself—that she was a long way from God and the road back to God was paved with repentance, revival, and revisioning.

Divine Appointments

The wise transitioning pastor must be alert to what can only be called "divine appointments." I was in east Tennessee doing a weekend conference at a church on the subject of disciple-making. The pastor had placed an article in the local paper promoting the event. I considered this rather odd, since the conference was designed mainly for the leaders of this particular church. About twenty-five people turned out for the three-day event. On Friday night, one individual attended who had seen the article in the paper. His name was Bill Carter.

Bill lingered after the meeting to talk. He said he was a retired United Methodist pastor and consultant who showed up because he was intrigued by the subject of the conference. He told me that he had other plans for Saturday night but would try to change them because he wanted to hear what else I had to say.

When he came the following night, he brought a book with him and presented it to me afterward. It was a book he had authored titled *Team Spirituality*. Later that night in my motel room, I opened the book and read a few pages. I was intrigued by what I read. It was about putting together a church staff, and we were getting ready to call another full-time staff person. Talk about divine appointments!

A few weeks later, I called Bill and we have had several conversations since then via email and telephone. I traveled back to east Tennessee about a year later and called Bill. We met for lunch, sitting for hours on a park bench in Jonesborough and chatting. I learned a lot from this "outside prophet" who came to me, I am convinced, through divine appointment. There have been numerous such appointments in the last few years.

Another example has been with a potter in Seagrove, North Carolina, a little town in the middle of the state known far and wide for its dozens of pottery shops. At a conference on discipleship, I met a potter named Tom Gray. Tom is a wonderful potter but also an interesting disciple. I traveled to Seagrove one day to meet with Tom. I found him in his potter's shop. I wondered if other visitors to Tom's pottery shop had been struck by the same feeling I had concerning the story in Jeremiah 18 about the prophet's visit to a potter's house. At the potter's house, Jeremiah was struck by the allegory of the potter as he shaped and reshaped the clay into something useful and good.

Tom and I have communicated about discipleship via email several times since that initial visit. At this point, I'm not sure which of us is supposed to the on the receiving end of this divine appointment. As a layperson, Tom has helped me gain a new perspective on what it means to be a disciple of Jesus Christ in the workplace and marketplace. I have learned valuable lessons in the "potter's house."

He has shared struggles with me concerning his church involvement and the call of God upon his life. Here is a quote from a recent email: "I look around and see a complacent body of Christ saying, 'Tom, what are you getting so stirred up about? What's wrong with the way things are?'" I often wonder if Tom's frustration is shared by a growing number of people in the body of Christ, people who are no longer content to sit and soak (and eventually sour) but who are asking the tough questions of church leadership concerning how they can get involved in making a difference in their world.

I am convinced that God had a hand in bringing us together, and I look forward to seeing how this relationship will unfold. At the bottom of his signature on his e-mails, Tom has this rather profound quote: "Who is the fool that says God has no right to add sand to our clay or marks to our vessel or fire to His workmanship? Who dares lift his clay fist heavenward and question the Potter's plan?"

Mentors

A lot has been said and written in recent years about mentoring. A relatively new term, "coaching," carries the same connotation. Actually, the concept of "Christian coaching" promises to be the new wave of the near future when it comes to helping people to achieve their goals and objectives.

One such mentor for me has been my old friend Wiley Rutledge. Wiley retired several years back from the active pastorate and now lives on a farm in east Tennessee. We got to be good friends during his twelve-year tenure at a nearby church. We hit it off instantly. Wiley thinks outside the box.

He has served as a tremendous source of encouragement to me. Going through years of transitioning can be stressful. About once a week, he and I would meet at a dumpy little restaurant for a chicken pita sandwich. We liked it prepared the exact same way—with grilled peppers and onions, extra peppers, and a generous pile of dill pickle chips on the side. Hold the fries—except when we were off our diet.

Wiley was never a critic. Maybe some mentors can fill that roll, but Wiley was my cheerleader. He told numerous people that if he were looking for a church to attend in the area, he would attend my church. Every pastor needs a Wiley, and this is especially true if they are in the work of transitioning a church.

An interesting footnote to Wiley is that he is a boyhood friend and lifelong acquaintance of one of my "book mentors" (see below), Bill Clemmons. The divine appointments at work here are startling. Findley Edge mentored Bill Clemmons, and the two of them mentored Eddie

Hammett at different times. Wiley Rutledge, a lifelong friend of Bill Clemmons, became my mentor and best friend. Jim Royston, who became the executive director of the Baptist State Convention of North Carolina, grew up listening to Wiley preach on the radio in Johnson City, Tennessee. Jim Royston, as it turns out, became Eddie Hammett's boss in his convention role. The beat goes on. Divine appointments are at work in the mentoring process as well.

The Power of the Printed Page

Before we began our transitioning process, I tried to read one book a year in its totality. There wasn't much time, you know, with keeping the institution alive and all. Now I feel like a failure if I don't read the equivalent of one book every week or two, plus numerous articles from journals and papers. It is a discipline I don't even want to think about trying to live without at this stage of my ministry.

Reading has helped sharpen the focus. It has helped open up a whole new world of ideas and experiences. Early in the transitioning process, one of our leadership teams read through a trilogy of books by Bill Hull, a pioneer in restoring the church to its disciple-making roots. The titles of those three books are *New Century Disciple Making, The Disciple-Making Pastor,* and *The Disciple-Making Church.*

The Power of the Group

Prophets come in different packages. We've already noted the prophet-in-person and the paperback varieties. There is one other prophetic resource without which I cannot function.

I'm referring to the support group. I'm not talking about a twelve-step program where the participants stand up and say, "Hello, my name is Ron and I'm a church flunkie." By support group, I simply mean a group of like-minded and opposite-minded individuals with whom you can be open and from whom you can get honest feedback. They need to be people who can challenge you and stretch you beyond where you presently are.

I always had a social group with whom I met on a weekly basis. Our meetings consisted of eating breakfast, drinking coffee, and chewing up all the ornery church members before belching and going back to the study. In retrospect, they were a drag on me and probably actually contributed to my depressed state.

In 1991, I joined a Clinical Pastoral Education (C.P.E.) group that met weekly for two semesters. There was nothing in the stated purpose of the group that would be a breeding ground for church reformers, but the group process gave me tremendous self-awareness. They helped me along the journey of reinventing myself, which would become a necessity for what I was about to do.

In summary, the support group is essential both for the church and for the pastor and other church leaders. I think this is especially true for leadership in churches going through a transitioning process. Such a group can serve a number of roles. They can be a sounding board for new ideas. They can give support and encouragement. They can tell the truth in love when one is off base. All church staff should be required to align themselves with a support group.

In recent years I have become part of a learning community. This is a group of pastors from a wide geographic region. We meet every six weeks to discuss the issues of transitioning churches. All of us pastor churches that have undergone and continue to undergo dramatic paradigm shifts. We meet to discuss these issues and how we are dealing with them.

We have made startling discoveries about ourselves in this learning community. One common experience is what we have named "battle fatigue." Most of us are physically, emotionally, and even spiritually exhausted. Pastoring a church in transition is taxing work. Sometimes it is like pastoring two churches—an old one and a new one—at the same time. We share our war stories. We give support and encouragement to each other. One of our members was fired by his church after four years of trying to move the church forward in a transitioning process. We were all devastated by this tragedy. There was a certain amount of fear and trepidation in all of us because deep inside, we all knew that it could happen to us the way it happened to Tom. He was fired without any warning and in the most unjust way imaginable. It was done by a church, God's agent of kindness and reconciliation. We were harshly reminded that all of us are engaged in spiritual warfare and that such warfare produces causalities.

Tom has found the group to be a source of help for him during this difficult time. Via e-mails and phone calls as well as face-to-face meetings, we gave Tom time to heal and share openly his pain and fears.

A New Reformation

It is interesting that Clemmons, Edge, and others like them have not been typical church program people. Findley Edge is the father of church renewal for many. His books *The Quest for Vitality in Religion* and *The Greening of the Church* remain as classics for anyone who believes the modern church has strayed from its New Testament purpose.

Actually, these spiritual giants have been leaders in an entire movement that is definitely afoot in the church as we begin the twenty-first century. Some have even called it a new reformation. Whereas the sixteenth century Protestant Reformation had taken God's Word out of the hands of the professional clergy and put it in the hands of the laity, this new reformation has a different slant. It seems to be progressing toward taking ministry out of the hands of the professional clergy and giving it back to the laity.

We had numerous outside prophets prior to Eddie Hammett. Revival speaker after revival speaker came to do their annual stirring up of the faithful. This agitation worked for a few days and sometimes a few weeks. Their evangelistic fervor managed to reach a few lost souls and shake up a few stagnant souls in the pews, but there was little lasting impact.

Choose the outside prophet carefully. Moses was a fellow Israelite, although he had been gone all those years. He understood their discontent. His story was the same as theirs, yet different. He could talk their talk, but he also held a vision before them that pulled them forward. He moved them off center.

How does a church choose an outside prophet? Collect résumés and do interviews until one is found? Hardly. Outside prophets, I believe, come to us by divine appointment. They come when people have prayed.

At some point in the early 1990s, a prayer group began to meet on Sunday morning before our Sunday school hour. Although this group was few in number, they were faithful to meet every week and pray for concerns in the church and for the renewal of the church. I believe their praying was absolutely essential for our church's renewal. They did not pray specifically for a prophet to come to us from the back side of some desert, but they prayed for the church and God heard their prayer. Sending outside prophets just happened to be one way God answered them.

After all, had not the children of Israel's deliverance from slavery in Egypt begun with prayer? That prayer had lasted for 400 years!

There Is Pow'r, Pow'r, Wonder-working Power

We had to learn to think outside the box. That's not easy when you made the box. We learn to make boxes well in church life. In Baptist life, we have programs such as Sunday school and W.M.U. and Brotherhood. These programs are good and were instrumental in shaping a whole denomination. Every denomination and every church has its own program boxes.

Renewal comes, however, when we begin to think outside the boxes. Institutions have a way of boxing us in. I have already described how the institution swallowed me. Being in the belly of the institution always seems to result from being disobedient to God. God had called me to pastor an open church—open to the gospel, open to the hordes of hurting and lost people all around it, open to the fresh winds of the Spirit, open to becoming involved where God was at work in the world. It was as if one day I was heaved upon the shore of this kind of church, freed at last from the belly of the great fish of church programs and maintenance.

I suppose the church will always have to fight institutionalism. Every generation will face its own battles in this arena. Christianity as an institution needs to die in our day and be reborn in new and fresh ways. It has been soiled and tainted by so much fingering and handling. I would have no trouble at all renouncing Christianity or even the church. It is my firm conviction that we should be followers of Jesus, not followers of a denomination or even a local church. Jesus was always bumping into organized religion. He gained followers precisely because he was willing to include them and free them and give them life. Often the church is not life-giving to those who need it the most.

In recent months, the Roman Catholic Church has been rocked by scandal. Some priests have been exposed as child molesters. This revelation has been enormously compounded by the fact that the church has been involved in covering up this travesty even in cases when they have known about it. What a scandal! They have been more concerned about keeping the institution viable than they have been about the children and others who have been harmed by the actions of a few priests.

Protestants have their own scandals in this area. My wife and I had dinner one evening with a couple in our church, Max and Amanda. I had married the couple years ago. I recalled the groom's parents and inquired about how they were doing. I also asked if Max and Amanda were attending the same church and how things were going at the church. Max replied that they were unhappy with their pastor, the reason being that he spent about two-thirds of his sermon berating the congregation for not attending the Sunday night and Wednesday night programs. The degree of hurt may not be the same as that of sexually molesting children, but the scandal is the same. This pastor is more concerned about the institution—the Sunday night and Wednesday night programs—than he is about the spiritual needs of people.

At Mission, we had to come to the place where we asked the hard questions about all of our programs. Discipleship became the litmus test for all we did, and we asked this question of our programs and ministries: "Does it make disciples? If it doesn't, it needs to be dropped or changed."

Streams in the Desert

Then will the lame leap like a deer, and the mute tongue shout for joy. Water will gush forth in the wilderness and streams in the desert. (Isaiah 35:6)

Early in the 1990s, we began to talk about the need for change. People were growing tired of oppressive church programs that seemed to produce so little in terms of church growth, numerically or spiritually. God began to hear our cries. A growing number of people began to get on board for an exodus. But not everyone was ready. There were murmurings. Murmurings never seem to go away where God's people are concerned.

"If we really want to set the children free, we will have to stay at it, and at it, and at it." This could have been Moses' theme song. Freedom does not come without costs, and one of the costs relates to persistence. There never comes a time in moving a church forward when we can say, "Okay, it's done. What project can we work on next?" All of this, of course, can be discouraging. At Mission, we faced times of great discouragement. Then God provided streams in the desert. Donna Gabbert first came to us in 1994. Her friend and coworker Marie was one of the people involved in the early days of church renewal. Along with many others, Marie, the mother of three teenaged boys, was dissatisfied that we were not providing enough spiritual growth opportunities for herself or her teens to become authentic followers of Jesus.

Marie had tried to witness to Donna for years. Donna came from a terribly dysfunctional family and was a victim of verbal and physical abuse as a child. Understandably, these experiences left deep emotional scars that she has carried into adulthood. She and her husband Richard were struggling in many ways, trying to raise two small children and trying to survive in the process.

We announced in fall 1995 that we were going to begin a support group called "Making Peace with Your Past." We would use a curriculum designed to help adult children of dysfunctional families. Marie invited Donna to join this group, offering to come with her although Marie herself did not come from a dysfunctional family.

Donna said no at first, but then she reluctantly agreed to come to the initial session. She had one condition: "Nobody better hug me or I won't come back." Marie promised and secretly prayed that no one would hug Donna. Donna had attended church periodically as a child. Every summer, her mother would ship her and her siblings off to whatever church was having Vacation Bible School. At practically every altar call after every Vacation Bible School, Donna would go forward and someone would help her pray the sinner's prayer, but no one ever followed up with her for discipleship. Her limited experience with church had left her distrustful and skeptic with regard to Christians and church people.

After the first session of "Making Peace with Your Past," Donna was hooked. By the end of the thirteen weeks she had begun to receive a lot of healing. She had also become the group's most enthusiastic hugger!

Though the details of her childhood abuse remained confidential within the group, her overall story had begun to filter out into the church body. By the time the group ended, Donna had begun to attend church regularly with her family, driving some twenty miles one way every Sunday and at least one other weeknight for her small group meeting.

About halfway into the group sessions, Donna gave birth to her third child. She had the baby on a Monday and came to the group session on Wednesday. Shortly after the group meetings ended, Donna was diagnosed with breast cancer. This is where her story really begins.

Over the next three years, Donna battled the cancer. In spring 1995, she made a profession of faith and was baptized. As she continued to battle cancer, the entire church rallied around her. Every Sunday morning when she was at worship, she would come down to the altar and kneel for prayer during the intercessory prayer time. Radiation and chemotherapy were taking their toll on her body, as was the cancer. She continued to come to church. Some Sundays there would hardly be a dry eye in the house as the congregation watched Richard help her to the altar and then back to her seat.

Donna succumbed to cancer on the Saturday before Easter in 1997. The legacy she left will be felt for a long time. A women's group planted a small flower garden on the church lawn with a small plaque that reads "In loving memory of Donna Gabbert." I suspect that garden will be there for a long time. We will not soon forget this courageous young mother who found healing and came to know Christ because our church dared to color outside the lines.

We learned from Donna that somehow we needed to design church for people who don't like to come to church. Donna taught us so much about ourselves, our mission, and what the future of our church could be.

Donna was just one such stream in the desert. Those who had resisted change were dwindling in number as Donna's story began to unfold. In spring 2001, the church held a banquet to kick off a capital funds campaign for a new building program. I asked Marie to be on the program to tell Donna's story. Even though most people had heard the story on numerous occasions, everyone was moved to tears once again as Marie recounted Donna's triumphant story.

Donna's story has become a powerful reminder of God's power to heal. Her story is also a reminder that when the church takes seriously the life of Jesus and decides to follow him, there will be countless stories like Donna's. Donna's spiritual transformation was documented in a beautiful poem written by her husband's aunt, JoAnn Fuhrman of Akron, Ohio.

> Blessed is she who suffered the ravishes of childhood abuse,
> and became loving.
> Blessed is she who was fearful of motherhood,
> and became a joy-filled parent, with Richard.
> Blessed is she who struggled to become a person of value in the workplace,
> and became the mentor and inspiration of fellow workers.
> Blessed is she who suffered the indignities of cancer and terrible pain,
> but fought with the heart of a lion, and found dignity.
> Blessed is she who questioned her own worth,
> and taught us to live in His grace,
> and inspired us to die in His service, with grace.
> Blessed is she who in her untimely death, taught us to live better.
> Fare thee well, lady of grace.

Spiritual renewal comes when God's people are willing to step outside their comfort zones and embark on a new journey. Murmurings are silenced when we dare to strike the rocks of resistance and stagnation so that waters of hope and new life gush forth.

Murmurings

What is the source of murmurings? They are the built-in resistance to change. William Bridges wrote about this extensively in his now-classic book, *Transitions*: ". . . they found it difficult to speak about the unexpected impact of an ending in their lives—and the way in which that unacknowledged ending stood in the way of moving forward successfully toward a new beginning."[5]

Change, no matter how helpful it may prove to be in the long run, shakes us out of our comfort zones. Not many of us like to be uncomfortable. We should expect resistance to any notion of change in the church. Israel was being delivered from 400 years of oppressive slavery.

They had no sooner gotten out of their bondage when some began to long for the "fleshpots of Egypt." Unbelievable, but predictable.

This is one discovery the instigators of change will not want to overlook. The dynamics of change are sure to sentence church leaders to many sleepless nights. We can be sure that murmurings will arise, and they will take unexpected forms.

Some people will want to go back to Egypt so strongly that they will attempt to wreak havoc in the church. Others will simply leave and go to another church. Make no mistake about it. These murmurings will come. One rather pessimistic friend of mine has concluded that people love comfort more than they love life. Is that too pessimistic a view? Most days I would agree that it is right on target. In Romans 7, Paul openly reveals part of the spiritual warfare that goes on within the soul of all of us. Most days it seems that the bad guys are winning. There has always been resistance to the Jesus way of doing church, and the more committed we are to his way, the more resistance we will encounter. Murmurings will happen. Count on it.

But understand this too—God can overcome the voices of discontent. He will do some remarkable things when his people embark on a journey to the promised land of renewal and hope. There are countless Donna Gabbert stories out there waiting to be told. These stories must be uncovered and told over and over if the church is to remain a viable and influential entity in the twenty-first century.

It would be generally agreed that in a broad sense all the baptized have a responsibility to transmit, interpret, and apply the Christian message within their own circumstances.[6]

Notes

[1] Oswald Chambers, *My Utmost for His Highest* (New York: Dodd, Mead & Company, 1935), 320.

[2] Robert Parham, "Moral Goodness," *Ethics Report* 9/3 (May/June 2001).

[3] Ibid.

[4] Eugene Peterson, *Under the Unpredictable Plant* (Grand Rapids MI: William B. Eerdmans , 1992), 18.

[5] William Bridges, *Transitions* (Reading MA: Addison-Wesley Publishing Company, 1980), 11.

[6] Geoffrey Wainwright, *Doxology: The Praise of God in Worship, Doctrine, and Life* (New York: Oxford University Press, 1980), 136.

Stirring the Waters

There is a lot of truth in the saying that the only person who likes change is a baby with a dirty diaper. Leaving a baby too long in a dirty diaper is never good. The result is usually a stinky mess or a painful rash or both. How do babies let us know they are uncomfortable? Since their communication skills are limited, about the only thing they know how to do is cry. This analogy may sound all too familiar to anyone who has a passion for transforming the church in our day.

It has often been estimated by church experts that as many as 75 percent of all churches presently in existence will close their doors in the next twenty-five years. The diapers are dirty. Do we love the church enough to roll up our sleeves and get to work with the unpleasant task at hand?

In Need of a Story

Church renewal needs many stories. The Bible is a chronology of God's renewing work in the lives of his people. We have already alluded to the renewal story of the exodus. There are others that worked for Mission.

The fifth chapter of John provided one of the great stories for our own situation. Jesus was in Jerusalem for a feast. Near the Sheep Gate was a pool called Bethesda. This was a favorite gathering place for those with physical disabilities. People on their way to the temple would pass by the pool. People on their way to a religious feast or other religious function usually consider hurting people to be something of a nuisance. For example, take the story of the Good Samaritan. The priest and Levite passed by the wounded man in their haste to get on with their religious duties.

Jesus saw an invalid man lying by the pool of Bethesda one day. Jesus not only saw him, but he stopped and asked him questions. He learned that the man had been in his paralyzed state for thirty-eight years. How many people had walked by him in thirty-eight years without even bothering to notice, let alone learn about him?

Paralysis can become an accepted condition. Now, 2,000 years later, most forms of paralysis still remain incurable. Church paralysis is never that hopeless. Churches can be renewed and restored. Churches can be made to walk again. Churches can be cleaned up and restored to a healthy condition.

There was a belief among the regulars at the pool that an angel would come down and stir the waters. When such stirrings occurred, it was believed that the lame and crippled could go into the water and have at least a chance at being healed. Of course, crippled people had a problem. They couldn't get into the water on their own. They had to depend on the mercy of others to help them.

Apparently there weren't many merciful people coming to the religious feast. When Jesus asked the man if he would like to be healed, he replied that he would, but there was no one to help him into the pool. Jesus immediately commanded him to take up his mat and walk.

Jesus was the one who stirred the waters for the man that day. He was always doing things in an unorthodox way. The religious authorities reacted to Jesus' mercy with disdain and disapproval. Why? Because he healed on the Sabbath. Jesus dared to tread on one of their sacred traditions.

Healing and restoring always requires a stirring of the waters. Frequently the church seems to be helpless to stir the waters on its own. It seems to suffer from a crippling paralysis. Why? Maybe it is too busy attending religious festivals. Indeed, the established church often resists the waters being stirred even at the risk of the hurting and lost being helped and saved. Note the reaction of established religious people to Jesus' healing of the invalid man. They wanted to throw the whole thing out on a technicality—namely, healing on the Sabbath.

Stagnancy and Stirring

Many stagnant church people do not want their waters stirred. The reasons are legion. It does little good to analyze and then rail against all the reasons. It is better to find creative ways to stir the waters of stagnation.

One effective way is through the telling and retelling of the Bible stories. Isaiah says that God's Word will not return to him empty. The Bible story is told most often in the pulpit. One of the biblical stories I told and continue to tell more than any other is the story of Jesus walking on the water, which is found in the Gospels. The early church must have found great comfort in this miracle story. They faced persecution from an established religious system as well as from an oppressive Roman Empire. The story of Jesus' disciples huddled in the boat amid a storm must have resonated with them. Jesus came to the disciples in the darkness of night walking on the water and invited them to get out of the boat and walk with him.

The disciples huddled in the boat in mortal fear can easily represent the modern church. We find church people today clinging to the boat, fearful to move one way or the other while the storms of secularism and consumerism rage on the outside. There is great comfort for many of them in the boat. There seems to be less danger of being smashed by the waves and less danger of sinking. The tendency of the church may be to stay huddled in the comparative safety of the boat, but Jesus bids us to come out of the boat and walk on the water with him. How can we hear the call of Jesus to get out of the boat?

Preaching stirs the waters like nothing else. I'm not talking about ranting and raving against the ills of the church and the stagnation of the people. The effectiveness of this kind of preaching is limited. Believe me, I have tried. First and foremost, being faithful to the biblical revelation means simply the retelling of the Gospel stories. They must be told over and over until they become like a mantra or the steady beat of the drum. They must be told and retold in creative and dynamic ways until the listener feels compelled to get out of the boat and walk on the water.

In our attempts to stir the waters at Mission, we also made judicious use of books and tapes. I would find a book that spoke to me and then pass it on to someone else. I spent hundreds of dollars, often out of my own pocket, to buy such books. People like Bill Easum, Tom Bandy, Bill Hull, Leonard Sweet, Michael Slaughter, Brian McLaren, Gene Wood, Lyle Schaler, Eddie Hammett, George Barna, and others are the modern-day prophets. Thankfully, they also write well and prolifically.

You can have the right vision, the right idea. You can even have the right result. But if you process it wrong, you'll have disaster.[1]

Notable Quotables

Sometimes I would glean a quotation from somewhere that spoke to our situation at the moment. I would post it on a wall or door or print it in the bulletin or newsletter. The printed word is a great water stirrer. One quotation came from Steve Arterburn in his book *Toxic Faith*. It read, "A terribly poisonous misconception is that God has a special calling for certain people and everyone else needs to find something unspecial to do."[2] That particular quote helped stir the waters of institutionalism.

Another one came from Bill Easum and Tom Bandy, coauthors of *Growing Spiritual Redwoods*. It read,

> "To whom do we really belong?" Christians belong both to Jesus and to the community. Our business is Jesus and community. To grow more like Jesus; to share what Jesus has done in our lives with others; to develop a community of love, hope, and trust in the midst of the yearnings of culture. That is our business. The purpose of any church is not merely to remember the story (the gospel), but to be and share the story (gospel).[3]

This profound little paragraph found its way to our website. A young man in our church, something of a computer whiz, came to me one day and asked if he could design and maintain a website for our church. I assented and he put it together in short order. In one of his early updates, he incorporated this quote, which I had printed in a Sunday worship bulletin, into our web site. More importantly, it would begin to become incorporated into the genetic code of the congregation.

Read, Read, Read

Hardly a committee meeting or ministry team meeting goes by that I don't hand out copies of an article from one or more journals and periodicals I subscribe to either online or in print. The pastor of the church under revision or renewal must become perhaps the most well-read person in the congregation. The sharp pen of prophetic utterance is mightier than the lifeless, stagnant waters of institutionalism and resistance to change.

I have four "branch libraries" in my life. Each is stocked with a few journals and magazines as well as a book or two. One of these branch libraries is the one in my home with the porcelain fixtures. Another one is my study at home. A third one is the most logical one, my study at church. The fourth one is in my car. No, I don't read while I'm driving and certainly don't recommend that. However, I sometimes eat lunch alone when I'm away from the office, and I always carry a book or journal with me. That way, I'm feeding my soul as well as my body. The time spent in waiting rooms is not wasted reading outdated copies of *Newsweek* or *Sports Illustrated*. Time in the waiting room time offers an opportunity to read a couple of articles in a journal.

I have also discovered coffee shops in recent years. A mid-morning or mid-afternoon coffee break at a Starbucks or another coffee shop can provide a cozy place to read a chapter or article. Coffee shops, by the way, are also a good place to observe a cultural phenomenon. I am amazed at the number of people who gather at such places for conversation and what we have traditionally in the church called fellowship. The church has much to learn from coffee shops about meeting the relational needs of people in our disconnected world.

Disturbing the Status Quo

"Stirring the waters" of discontent simply means to help people begin thinking outside the box and coloring outside the lines. It means disturbing the *status quo*, which does not always make the pastor or church leader the most popular person in the universe. Stories abound about pastors who dared to stir the waters and were fired and literally thrown out on the street. As Kathleen Norris aptly stated, "There is both irony and schism built into a system that uses expulsion as a means of preserving its unity."[4]

The transitioning pastor, however, sees this stirring of the waters as part of his/her prophetic role. From the biblical revelation, we draw the conclusion that God is never satisfied with the *status quo*. If he were, prophets would have been unnecessary. The great apostles like Paul, Peter, and John would have had much different ministries, and the stories told about them would not be the same.

Imagine what would have happened if Jesus himself had been satisfied with the calm waters of religious tradition. The story of Jesus stirring the waters in Luke 5 is a powerful metaphor of his entire life and ministry. It got him into trouble with the authorities and eventually led to his execution.

Stirring the waters disturbs people. It creates messes and takes things apart that can never be returned to their previous state. The life of the lame man at the pool of Bethesda was changed forever. The power of God was unleashed in his life in the person of Jesus. When we begin to stir the water, we have no idea how any of this will end up.

Friends in Low Places

"Stirring the waters" also means finding positive power even in negative emotions. My depressed state in the late 1980s would actually become my friend. A friend of mine, Tom O'Neil, a professional counselor, wrote to me after I took a Clinical Pastoral Education course he led. I still have the letter. In the letter, he spoke of my depression and said that "Ronny has found depression to be his friend. I am confident that in the future he will recognize when it is coming and actually use it to his advantage."

Depression as a friend? Jeffery Smith wrote of depression's devastation: "Depression robs whatever present-day pleasure we're accustomed to deriving from them, and the future, to the depressed person, looks like nothing other than an endless loop of now."[5] However, my friend Tom isn't the only one to recognize the positive power of depression. Therapists have written about it. I have come to believe that depression and other symptoms of a troubled spirit are often God's way of getting our attention and encouraging us to travel into the soul in a quest for deeper meaning.

Some of the early church fathers wrote about the "dark night of the soul." This journey into darkness enables the soil of the soul to be tilled and disturbed so that seeds of hope can germinate and eventually bear fruit.[6]

My discouraged and depressed state would lead me to work hard in the future to avoid that kind of melancholy. God has indeed used all of those negative emotions for good in my personal life.

Bubble-up People

I do not believe church renewal can take place without one key ingredient strategically deployed. I am talking about what I call the remnant group. Early in our transitioning process, I began to gather people together in a small group setting. We used Henry Blackaby's *Experiencing God* as our curriculum, but it could have been any number of curriculum pieces. The most effective small groups, I believe, are relationship-driven, not curriculum-driven.

Who should compose such a group? I was careful to print an invitation in the Sunday bulletin that the group was open to anyone. However, most old paradigm church people would not be interested. Most group participants were personally invited. It is important to invite people who think outside the box. It is no accident that Jesus used this strategy when gathering that remnant group of twelve around him.

From what I have observed, a prerequisite for pastors to lead a church through transitioning seems to be that they are at least slightly mentally unstable. I was invited to a gathering of "innovative church leaders" convened by my state denomination. It didn't take me long to realize that I was in a room full of "unbalanced" people. I mean that in a good way, of course. Then it dawned on me that I was one of them!

Isn't this the way Jesus did it? There was not a religious traditionalist among the Twelve. They were "remnant" people, nonconformists, untrained in church matters, unbalanced and unstable. What did Jesus do with this ragtag group? He only invested three years of his life in them.

An intimate small group won't develop overnight, nor will it happen in a twelve-week workbook study. In 1995 I gathered fourteen people together and we spent a year going through several workbooks. Along the way I also trained them to become small group leaders. When the year was over, we then deployed many of the fourteen as small group leaders themselves. That became the foundation for our small group ministry. I also believe it laid the groundwork for the spiritual revolution that would take place in our church. A quote from leadership guru John Maxwell has stuck in my mind. Though I can't recall the source, he said, "Grow a person and everything around that person grows."

Even now, six years later, I lead a small group. My present group is the fourth group in which I have invested at least a year of coaching and teaching and continuing to stir the waters.

Where do you find such people? I can only say that they will "bubble up" when you begin to stir the waters. Most of them will not be among the present church leadership. It isn't that they lack leadership ability or potential. It is likely that they have not been asked, primarily because they were perceived as being nonconformists.

Look for these "unbalanced" people. Pray for them to bubble up. There are still some in every congregation, although most of them have probably become dropouts due to being isolated and not encouraged. Look back over the past couple of years and make a list of the dropouts. Are any among this group candidates for a new leadership group? Probably so. Why not contact them and see what happens?

Not all of the "bubble-up" people will follow through. We had one such lady. She seemed to fit the unstable mold, but she proved to be too much so. Accountability must be built into small groups. A small group cannot function without it. Making disciples cannot take place without it. I'm talking about accountability in the context of loving and caring relationships within the group. Group members must be accountable to each other to be and do what they say they are going to be and do. In this way, they help each other keep their commitments.

The lady of whom I speak could not handle the responsibility. Sometimes there is a fine line between reckless commitment and plain irresponsibility. However, this is not a reason to look at everyone with suspicion. Invite them anyway. Take chances on people. Jesus certainly did this with his remnant bunch. One of them, Judas Iscariot, went over the edge on the side of irresponsibility. Simon Peter teetered there, but Jesus loved him back into the fold.

We tried to work with the lady, but she was not ready to take the journey with us. She and her husband eventually left our church and became active in another church where they have become leaders. I was disappointed because I thought she had much potential for the vision we were developing.

Oh, the Places You'll Go

These early experiences with the bubble-up people will take you to faraway places. Oh, the stories you'll have to tell. Actually, the whole business of transitioning is a return to the biblical story. God's people in the Bible are always on the move. The two greatest events in the Old Testament are about remnant people leading Israel across desert sands in search of a sacred place. The exodus and the exile are not about people living in stability.

Rita was one of our remnant people. It was evident early in our transitioning process that someone had stirred her waters. She had a healthy dissatisfaction with the way things were. Uniquely gifted to stir the waters for others, she became an important cog in our transition wheel.

I think of Rita as a grenade tosser. She even made me nervous at first until I learned to stay in the background and allow the grenades to do their work. Sometimes I would have to bind up the wounded in the paths of her grenades, but my pastoral skills were well-suited for the task. We actually made a great team in that respect. Rita did not possess the spiritual gift of mercy, and so she would plow ahead with a project until its completion. Mercy is high on my list of spiritual gifts, and so I would be there to soothe and bind the wounded, while at the same time giving encouragement to Rita to keeping tossing those grenades.

Messiness Rules

Messiness is something the transitioning pastor will have to get used to. I have found that remnant people often lack gifts of mercy. They have a tendency to ignore feelings and go for results. It's not that they don't care about feelings, but like the biblical prophets, they are results-oriented people. They are grenade tossers. The bottom line is that remnant people must be allowed to do their work. Let someone else pick up the pieces and bind the wounded.

The messiness comes when the grenades are tossed and the debris flies all over the place. I'm not suggesting that people must be hurt in the process of transitioning. Things can be done to minimize the number of hurt people, and no one should ever be hurt intentionally. However, some will choose to claim the hurt for themselves. This, I think, is inevitable.

The wise pastor will coach these grenade tossers to be prepared for criticism of the worst kind. They are actually less likely to be deterred by harsh criticism than the pastor. Most pastors are people who want to be liked and possess the spiritual gifts of mercy and other gifts associated with compassion. Grenade tossers, who often lack the gifts of mercy and compassion, can be teamed with mercy people to minimize the "collateral damage" of their grenades. Tom Bandy wrote:

> Traditional clergy do tend to be more handicapped in organizational transformation in contrast to the entrepreneurship of their business, education, and nonprofit lay leaders. It is not just that they cannot curse when they make mistakes. The problem is they cannot make mistakes, behave aggressively, or act daringly without incredible guilt and anxiety. Traditional clergy were raised in peace, trained in conflict resolution, and certified to build unity. Their career path cannot tolerate chaos. When modern clergy become post-modern coaches, their walk is the walk of an "overwrought soul."[7]

At some point in our transitioning process, we determined that we needed to have a church logo. Darrell Williams, our Minister of Discipleship and Leadership Development, and I put our heads together and came up with an idea. For the front cover of a discipleship workbook we used often in small groups, an artist had rendered a picture Jesus with a handful disciples on a boat in the Sea of Galilee. In the picture, Jesus is talking to the small band of disciples, who are looking on with keen interest. It has become my conviction that this picture captures the essence of the Christian faith—disciples spending time alone with Jesus in an isolated place, learning at the feet of the Master.

The sea can be an isolated place, but it can also be a dangerous place. We are familiar with the Gospel stories about storms on the sea and the calming presence of Jesus to alleviate fears and give courage to the sometimes timid and anxious followers. During such storms and crises, faith is strengthened and hope is renewed. The imagery of Psalm 107:23 has become a metaphor for our church in its quest for spiritual vitality. It reads, "Some went down to the sea in ships, doing business on the great waters; they saw the deeds of the LORD, his wondrous works in the deep" (RSV). The psalmist seems to be saying that in the deep waters, we really find God; we see his "deeds" and "wondrous works." Out of the dangerous and sometimes chaotic conditions of the deep water, we see works of God that cannot be seen in any other place.

Soon, we began to think of the image of a sailboat as a church logo. A sailboat cannot move on its own power. It is dependent on the wind to get to its destination. Likewise, the church cannot rely on its own power. The church must depend on the wind that is the Spirit of God. In Hebrew, the words wind and spirit are from the same root word. A boat stirs the waters as it moves forward toward its destination. Only when the boat is anchored and not moving forward can it expect the waters to be calm.

We submitted our idea to Gary Veazey, a graphic designer. He came up with our sailboat logo with the phrase "a church that cares." To say we are a church that cares is moving into deep waters. It means we had better be prepared to back it up with actions.

Deep waters are not safe, and they are not manageable. The transitioning church should be prepared for danger and chaos. Out of the chaos, creation takes place. Eugene Peterson wrote, "Mess is the precondition of creativity. Creativity is not neat. It is not orderly. When we are being creative we don't know what is going to happen next. When we are being creative a great deal of what we do is wrong."[8] Albert Einstein used these rules of work:

• One: Out of clutter, find simplicity.
• Two: From discord, find harmony.
• Three: In the middle of difficulty lies opportunity.[9]

Those are good rules to apply in the transitioning church. With all those "bubble-up people" and "grenade tossers," there will be clutter, discord, and difficulty. Messiness rules, but out of the messiness and chaos God can create something new. He always has.

That's why it is important to continually cast the vision in the transitioning church. The pastor/coach must learn to see the big picture and constantly keep it before the whole congregation as well as the remnant people. In the dark days of World War II, England was bombed relentlessly by Germany. More than 50,000 people lost their lives in the bombings. Prime Minister Winston Churchill was often found walking among the ruins from the previous night's bombing. He was there to cast the vision, help the people to see the big picture amid the chaos and ruins, and move forward to victory. Historians credit Churchill's "coaching" through these critical times as one of the reasons England eventually prevailed over their enemy. Coaching is a good term for the kind of leadership needed in the chaos and messiness of a church transitioning from stagnation to vitality.

Casting the Vision

Once stirred and then left undisturbed, waters return to their original placid state. They must be stirred again and again. I call it casting the vision, and it must be done repeatedly. There are numerous opportunities in church life where the waters can be stirred.

(1) The pulpit. God's Word is filled with examples of renewal. Renewal is the essence of the gospel itself. Good news for the believer means receiving a second chance. It means being regenerated; it means being reclaimed and redeemed by a forgiving and renewing God. Preaching to a church in transition must involve applying the truths of the Bible to the journey shared together.

(2) Weekly publications. Most churches have a weekly communication called the Sunday bulletin. At Mission, we call it the worship folder. The weekly worship folder is a place where vision can be communicated. Most churches and pastors don't realize what a wonderful opportunity the weekly bulletin presents.

(3) Other publications. We publish a monthly newsletter. The cost of mailing a newsletter is virtually nothing compared to the return on the investment. They cost pennies each to mail. We send them to everyone—from first-time visitors to former members who moved away eight years ago. I always write a column in the newsletter, and 90 percent of the time it is about the church's vision. My church members expect me to push the envelope at least a little in my monthly column. It is a place where I can choose my words carefully and lead the church at least to think outside the lines.

(4) Committee meetings. We have reduced committees to a minimum, and we are in the process of converting most of them to teams. Regardless of the form they take, these groups provide another important place to share the vision. Never allow a meeting to convene without mentioning the church's vision—where you're going, the progress you're making in getting there, what adjustments need to be made along the way, etc.

(5) Staff meetings. It doesn't matter if the church staff consists of twenty people or two people. Staff meetings are yet another opportunity to stir the vision waters. In setting the agenda, the senior pastor should always include something about the vision. A staff meeting may consist of nothing more than the single pastor chatting with the janitor in front of the supply closet on Monday morning. It doesn't matter. Cast the vision.

(6) Share the stories. Stories of lives transformed are constantly emerging in the transitioning church. Some of them are personal and must be kept confidential. Others can and should be shared. They can be shared in every forum from private conversations to public declarations. One effective place to share the stories is in the sermon. Nothing illustrates a sermon better than the three-to-five-minute faith story from someone whose life is being transformed by the power of God.

(7) Symbols. Every church has symbols. They may not be utilized, but they are there. From the building design to the church stationery, they all are tools of communication. I've already mentioned the sailboat in our church

logo. These symbols communicate something, whether intentionally or not.

(8) Conversations. Do not underestimate the power of conversations with church parishioners as an effective tool for casting the vision. Remember that conversation involves both speaking and listening. The pastor of a transitioning church needs to spend time talking to people over coffee or lunch or ice cream. The personal time spent with an individual can be more powerful than preaching to hundreds when it comes to casting the vision.

Jesus was the master vision caster. He did it in unconventional ways. Here are a few I have gleaned from the Gospel accounts:

• Jesus was a risk taker. He always seemed to live on the edge. In Luke 4, the angry crowd takes him literally to the edge and threatens to throw him off the precipice. Jesus always seemed to be running afoul of others and their agendas. Yet, in a calculated way, he was willing to take the risk. Vision casters must be risk takers.

• Jesus used the concept of servant leadership. He was willing to take up the basin and the towel and humble himself before even his followers. This kind of leadership inspires greatness in others.

• Jesus was a team builder. The disciples were a team. Jesus constantly worked at ways to mold them into an effective group of visionary followers.

• Jesus was an investor. Have you ever stopped to consider how much time Jesus invested in a few people? Jesus never truly discipled the masses. He preached to the crowds and healed their sick, but he invested his life in a few. These few, the Twelve, turned the world upside down. Sometimes it was a conversation with one person that cast the vision for the masses. That kind of investment in a few people pays huge dividends.

• Jesus was focused. In Luke 19:10, Jesus sets his face resolutely to go to Jerusalem. Nothing could deter him from his mission. In John 10:10, Jesus says, "I have come that you might have life in all of its abundance." Jesus knew his life's mission. He knew who he was and what his ministry was all about. Casting the vision requires a steady focus.

Stirring the waters helps create a readiness for change. Without this readiness, efforts at change and transition will be futile. Church consultant George Bullard says that if a sense of readiness and urgency has not been created, then it is probably useless to try to bring about change.[10]

Do not try to bypass the step of "stirring the waters" in moving a church from a state of stagnancy to renewal and vitality. Find out where the stage of paralysis is and begin to stir the waters of complacency and apathy. Healing will not always occur instantly. Sometimes, remarkably, it will. Most often, however, it will take weeks, months, or even years. Pack a lunch and be prepared for the long haul.

Notes

[1] Lon Solomon, interview for *Leadership: A Practical Journal for Church Leaders* (summer 2000), 26.

[2] Stephen Arberburn & Jack Felton, *Toxic Faith: Understanding and Overcoming Religious Addiction* (Nashville TN: Oliver-Nelson Books, 1991), 165.

[3] Tom Bandy and Bill Easum, *Growing Spiritual Redwoods* (Nashville TN: Abingdon Press, 1997), 16.

[4] Kathleen Norris, *Dakota: A Spiritual Geography* (New York: Houghton Mifflin Company), 59.

[5] Jeffery Smith, *Where the Roots Reach for Water: A Personal & Natural History of Melancholia* (New York: North Point Press), 21.

[6] Ronald Peterson, *Faith@Work* (fall 2000), 13

[7] Tom Bandy, *Coaching Change* (Nashville: Abingdon Press, 2000), 164.

[8] Eugene Peterson, *Under the Unpredictable Plant: An Exploration in Vocational Holiness* (Grand Rapids MI: William B. Eerdmans Publishing Company), 163.

[9] Phil Jackson and Hugh Delehanty, *Sacred Hoops* (New York: Hyperion, 1995), 70.

[10] George Bullard, *Net Results* (July 2000), 28.

Counting the Cost

Change isn't painful. Resistance to change is painful. (author unknown)

In seminary I had taken a course titled Church Administration. It was taught by a visiting professor who was a denominational employee for much of his ministry. He said something I have never forgotten: "If you are going to become a martyr, make sure it is something worth dying for."

Much of what we "die for" in our churches is, quite honestly, not worth it. My wife and I built a house a couple of years ago. People warned us that building a house together would be a severe test for our marriage. There were stressful times, but they weren't as trying as most people predicted. Why? I think the reason was simple. I allowed my wife to make most of the design and decorating decisions. There weren't many hills I was willing to die on when it came to choosing colors and materials. It's not that I didn't care. It's not that I didn't have some strong convictions about what I wanted. I voiced my opinions, but in the end I learned to say with all humiliation, "Yes dear, I think that would look nice." We got along fine.

Compare this to the hills on which many pastors die. Most church fights are over issues that matter little when it comes to the Kingdom of God. Does it really matter to God whether the carpet is green or blue or whether the children have Kool-Aid™ or a popular soft drink at Vacation Bible School? Most confrontations can be avoided by deciding in the beginning which hills are worth dying on. There better not be many such hills, or the pastor will die a thousand deaths.

See a Hill, Take a Hill

The call came from Don, the pastor of a church in Texas. He had heard about our church's revisioning process resulting in revitalization. He had questions. Don is an ex-Marine. By his own admission, he was not the most tactful pastoral leader. His *modus operandi* was, in his words, "See a hill, take a hill." He recounted a number of church fights that had occurred in his congregation during the past couple of years. I reminded him that one can also die just trying to take a hill.

Which church hills are worth dying for? Not many.

This is where a mission statement and a set of core values and beliefs become essential for the revisioning church. What should be the mission of the church? Say it any way you want, but Jesus gave us the marching orders for the church. It is found in Matthew 28 and is generally known as the Great Commission. Any mission statement that does not have making disciples at its heart is, biblically speaking, an inferior mission statement.

A Decisive Destination

More will be said about mission, vision, and beliefs in a later chapter, but suffice it to say here that the revisioning church must know where it is going. A clear sense of direction helps a church stay focused on the essentials.

Once that is determined, the next step is to count the cost involved in moving toward that end. In Luke 14:28-30, Jesus teaches about counting the cost. He asks, "Suppose one of you wants to build a tower. Will he not first sit down and estimate the cost to see if he has enough money to complete it?" (NIV).

Now, suppose one of you wants to revitalize and transition a church? Should you not first sit down and count the cost to see if you have enough spiritual energy and other resources to complete the job?

We cannot possibly know what this revitalized church is going to look like when it is completed, so we cannot possibly know the full costs involved. However, we can understand that there will be costs. Do not think for a moment that you can transform a church without messiness, chaos, conflict, and pain. We would do well to heed the warning of Jesus at this point.

500 What?

At ministerial gatherings, you can hear numerous conversations that begin with the question, "How are things going?" The replies are predictable. "Great, we had over 500 in worship Sunday," or "God is really blessing us; we're averaging around 450 in Sunday school." Nobody ever asks, "500 what?" Our emphasis on and sometimes obsession with numbers causes us to lose sight of the real mission of the church, which is to make disciples.

Churches that grow rapidly in numbers should have more than a little concern about how they disciple new converts. Jesus never said, "Go and make believers or converts." He said, "Go and make disciples."

After Jesus had preached and fed the 5,000, something strange happened. He talked about sacrifice and denial, and they all began to fall away. Only the Twelve were left. Jesus asked them if they also were going away, and their response was that they didn't have any place left to go. Jesus fully embodied their hope and dream for a new life.

One of the costs of church revisioning and transitioning is to understand that some will leave. Sometimes they will leave in droves; sometimes in a trickle. You will probably feel hurt by everyone who leaves, at least for a while. In his book *Transitioning*, Dan Southerland quotes Bill Hybels as saying, "You only have enough tears for one group: those who are walking toward you or those who are walking away from you. Choose whom you will weep over."[1]

That statement may sound callous. Some may read it and say, "Well, that's okay for them to say. They have thousands of people. So what does it hurt if a few dozen or even a few hundred walk away?" It is difficult in a church of 100 or even 300 to watch people walk away. Usually these are people in whom a pastor and others have invested time and energy. Ministers may have celebrated with those people the birth of children or grandchildren, mourned the death of loved ones, played golf, eaten dinner, and counted them among their best friends. This has happened more than once at Mission, and let me tell you it hurts every time. One such couple was Harry and Dawn. They left with no explanation other than a few very weak excuses. I talked to them at length, and they could offer no plausible reason for wanting to leave our church. This has been almost two years ago, and I still don't have a real clue. Sometimes people just leave, and they really aren't able to articulate why. I suspect they know but feel embarrassed to tell.

When we made a clear decision to embark on a journey to become a disciple-making church, we raised the bar quite a bit for some people. We began to talk about things like accountability in the context of loving relationships. We began to talk frequently about spiritual disciplines such as Bible study, prayer, quiet time, evangelism, worship, fasting, and other things. I have come to believe that most of the people who left our church, and many of them had been in positions of leadership, left because the spotlight of discipleship was turned on them, and they knew they were not willing to be revealed for what they were—weak and immature in their walk with the Lord. We cannot expect everyone to complete the journey. "Sometimes God gives us individuals and groups who have the ability to hike only a portion of the trail, so to speak."[2]

Harry and Dawn were two of those people with whom my wife and I had become close friends. We had shared table fellowship many times. Harry and I had gone hiking together and on spiritual retreats together. It hurt for a long time when they left. Count the cost of building a disciple-making church!

Where Will They Go?

Some who leave will go to other churches that are less demanding and ask for less commitment. Some will drop out of church altogether. Some will get mad and leave over something trivial. One couple who left offered a reason so revealing of their immaturity that it was almost laughable. The husband was leading a particular ministry in our church. When we talked about getting more people involved in her ministry, he became offended that we wanted to take his ministry away from him and so he went to another church. I'm not making this up. At last check, several years after he left, he and his wife were simply attending worship at another church and had no involvement beyond that one hour on Sunday morning. Casual Christianity is an anemic brand of the faith, but it does have its appeal.

Flamingo Road in Fort Lauderdale, Florida, was another story. In writing about their story, Dan Southerland talks about losing 300 people in 9 years! He describes them as people who could not handle the changes. That amounts to about half the people who were there when the transition began. He is also quick to point out that the church gained more than 2,000 in the same time period. "We have lost three hundred that were already committed to Christ—and gained two thousand, most of whom were unchurched, lost, and going to hell."[3]

The First Baptist Church of Spartanburg has a similar story. At a pastor's conference, Pastor Don told the heartbreaking story of losing scores of people who could simply not handle change. Such losses are enough to scare away the timid and fearful from even wanting to move a church through major changes.

White Oak Baptist Church was a small rural congregation in the middle of a bludgeoning suburban sprawl near Raleigh, North Carolina. For decades it had been planted in the middle of a rural community called Archer's Lodge just outside of Clayton, about 25 miles east of Raleigh. When the community began to change, the church faced a choice— change or die. Under the leadership of John Mark Batchelor, they chose to change. Some of the old paradigm people could not stand the change and so they left. They didn't leave by the hundreds because the church never had more than two hundred before transitioning began. They did lose about twenty-five people in one year, which was a significant number considering the proportions.

Our losses were minimal. Over a period of ten years, we have probably had no more than forty people to abandon ship. As already stated, each of the losses was painful. In a few cases, their leaving was like a breath of fresh air because they resisted change so strongly, but in most cases I felt a sense of loss. Pastor Bill Hybel's words about not having enough tears for both those coming and going have been of some solace to me, but like most pastors I still like to think I have enough compassion for all of God's children.

Gordon Cosby, founding pastor of Church of the Savior in Washington, DC, has these words of wisdom:

> We must come to the place where we can do what Jesus did, where we can watch the rich young ruler walk away and, with sorrow and an ache in our hearts, let him go until he can come back on the terms of Jesus Christ. We have been so afraid we might lose potential members that we have been willing to take them on their own terms. Then we wonder why the church is relatively impotent and doesn't have the power to transform human life, to shake society to its very roots.[4]

We would all do well to remember that Jesus also lost many followers over the course of his earthly ministry. Raymond Bailey offers a wonderful insight on this point.

> His [Jesus'] listeners often were disturbed by what He said and left disagreeing with His conclusions or rejecting His solutions, but they recognized the everyday language and were confronted by concrete application and clear expression. Most of those who went away did not withdraw because of confusion; they turned away because they understood exactly what He was saying and could not believe it or would not yield to the demands of His message.[5]

This Train Is Bound for Glory, This Train . . .

I like to use the train metaphor to describe what happens when a church moves through change. Perceive the church as a giant passenger train rambling down the tracks. Everything is fine as long as the train is on time and on track. Then some of the passengers begin to get a suspicious feeling that the train is headed in the wrong direction. They talk to a few other passengers. Pretty soon they too become convinced that the train is going in the wrong direction.

The number of malcontents grows. They consult those in charge of running the train. Finally, most of those on the train are convinced that the train is indeed going the wrong way. The first move is to get the train stopped, which is certainly no easy task. The bigger the train, the more time it takes to slow it down. Some people resist the notion of turning the train around in the first place. Some of them jump off the train at the earliest and safest moment. Some of them would rather wreck the train than allow its direction to be altered.

Finally the train is stopped. Some get off at this point, unconvinced that the train is actually headed in the wrong direction. They will wait at the station for the next train. Stopping the train takes a lot of energy, but so does turning it around. It isn't easy to turn around a huge freight train. Sometimes the engine has to be changed.

There is something exciting about a train station. People hear that a train is going their way and they jump on board. There is initial excitement among the old passengers as new passengers join them. The disgruntled passengers who got off earlier are replaced by new people with a new excitement. Some of them are simply glad to be going anywhere, and others have a real sense of a specific destination.

Now those in charge of leading the train say that if the train ever gets to where it is going, there will have to be changes. There must be a deeper commitment to get to this new destination. Much time has been lost, so it will take a long time to get the train to its desired destination. Newcomers will have to be acclimated. The people who have been on the train for a long time will have to learn to live with these newcomers, who have new and sometimes radical ideas. It won't be easy. Some cannot stand the changes that inevitably result, and so they get off at the next stop.

New people board the train at every opportunity. The old guard who was on the train for so long, who saw the train go through dark tunnels and terrible storms, now feels that the train, although headed in the right direction, has forgotten him. New food is served in the dining car. New, jazzy music plays, and there is a new dance the old passengers have never seen before. Some of the longtime passengers never danced at all.

What I have described is part of the cost of moving from a maintenance church to a mission church. Those accustomed to quiet order on the train where the wait staff is dressed in neat, starched uniforms, are in for a rude awakening.

When a church starts to make authentic disciples or what Mike Slaughter calls "real followers," you can be sure many will rise up in protest. In Philippians 2:4-8 Paul wrote, *look not only to your own interests, but also to the interests of others. Your attitude should be the same as that of Christ Jesus: Who, being in very nature God, did not consider equality with*

God something to be grasped, but made Himself nothing, taking the very nature of a servant, being made in human likeness. And being found in appearance as a man, He humbled Himself and became obedient to death—even death on a cross!

I can promise you that if you introduce that kind of servant attitude into the life of a church, it will radically change the church's character. Some people won't like it. Looking to the interests of others is counter-cultural. Popular culture says to look out for number one. Those in positions of leadership in most churches are typically those who hold positions of leadership in industry and business. Sometimes they can even be described as high-powered executives accustomed to barking orders and expecting immediate results. The disciple-making church will not respond to that kind of leadership. Disciples of Jesus Christ ask first about the feelings of others and embody humility and servanthood.

Three Distinctives

I would like to identify three distinctives that separate the disciple-making church from ordinary churches. The culture created by a disciple-making church runs counter to the views of people accustomed to another paradigm. This will cause conflict that to some degree cannot be avoided, but it can be minimized.

The disciple-making church is mission-driven. A disciple-making church is literally on a "mission from God." In the now classic movie *The Blues Brothers,* the two brothers played by Dan Akyrod and John Belushi describe their mission as "a mission from God." Actually they use this as cover for their less-than-godly antics. The disciple-making church understands that its mission is to serve God by making disciples. Church consultant George Bullard identifies this commitment to adult discipleship development as one of the key factors that empowers redevelopment in a church: "If the congregational leaders are on a personal spiritual strategic journey to deepen the dimensions of their own discipleship, then transformation is more likely. They are also likely to create opportunities for others to grow as disciples."[6]

The church has no mission or purpose other than to make disciples. We do not exist to be a social club, provide recreation for our members, or be a place to network for business. Neither do we exist only to worship, study the Bible, or do evangelism. These things are secondary to our primary mission, which is to make disciples. The disciple worships, studies the Bible, shares his or her faith, and may even socialize, enjoy recreation and fellowship, and network along the way, but none of these is the primary purpose of the church. The disciple-making church is mission-driven. One thing is certain, although perhaps surprising to some: many people will not like this kind of church. They prefer a church that isn't quite so focused and clear about its purpose.

The mission-driven church asks constantly of every activity and organization: "What is its disciple-making function?" Try asking that of the women's group or men's group that has met once a month primarily for fellowship and coffee since the Roosevelt administration (Teddy), and you will shake things up. Don't say I didn't warn you.

Secondly, the disciple-making church is ministry-based. If a disciple is an authentic follower of Jesus Christ, he or she will be involved in ministry. Why? Simple. That's what Jesus did. Jesus was involved, for example, in healing. No, I'm not advocating that you get up a busload to attend a Benny Hinn crusade. We involve ourselves in the ministry of healing when we befriend the addict, the prison inmate, the homeless, the sick, the poor. This ministry includes hospital visits, prayer, and especially direct involvement in the lives of hurting people. "The church must unleash the Good News, the power of Christ, and the mission of the church outside the programs and walls of the church. Until we commission and bless Christian leaders to follow Christ's calling into the world, we will continue to build an institutional faith that limits the power and presence of the gospel faith."[7]

When a church begins to heal the hurting, you can be sure those who hurt in the community will find out about it. What's more, they will begin to come to church. The ministry-driven church needs to count the cost of being a church that attracts hurting people. Their hurts won't be the same hurts of nice church-going people. Their hurts will not be as hidden like those of most lifelong church people, who often hide their hurts rather than reveal them and risk humiliation and shame.

One Sunday morning during greeting time in worship, I turned around after shaking a worshiper's hand to find myself face to face with a stranger. I reached out my hand to take his, and I will never forget his first words: "Can I stay?" His eyes were a bit glassy, and there was the slight smell of alcohol on his breath. "Of course you can stay," I muttered, taken a bit off-guard by his abrupt and unusual question. He introduced himself to me as Marty. What he said next was equally stunning. "I just want to find Jesus," he said. "Brother," I said with confidence, "you have come to the right place."

I motioned for one of our deacons sitting nearby to come over and asked him to sit with Marty during the service. I don't know what brought this poor soul to our church that morning, but I know there was a world of hurt there. After the service I spent time with Marty, and he begin to tell his story. When we sat down in my office and I closed the door behind me, I turned to Marty and asked, "How long have you had a drinking problem?"

"I knew that you knew," he said. Indeed, he had the look of a man who had been on a weekend binge, not a man who had consumed a couple of beers.

At my encouragement and insistence, Marty enrolled in a twelve-step program and continued to attend worship occasionally. He has taken steps to recovery but still has a long journey. A ministry-based church will attract hurting people, and this will make many uncomfortable. Many people prefer a nice, placid little church filled with folks "just like us." Michael Yaconelli puts it this way: "Nothing makes people in the church more angry than grace."[8]

Three ladies involved in one aspect of our youth ministry caught me after a meeting at church one night and asked if they could speak with me for a few minutes. They were frustrated because they had been working on a creative movement piece for four months but the unruly behavior of the fifteen youth had prevented them from making progress. Some of the youth had been rude, disrespectful, and disruptive. Furthermore, there were reports of less-than-Christlike behavior in the parking lot after a rehearsal. The three women were discouraged. We talked for a while and devised a couple of strategies to deal with the problem, but I mainly tried to get them to see the big picture. I reminded them that a church on mission to the unchurched in the community would have this kind of messiness. Messiness rules in the mission-oriented church! Get used to it.

Thirdly, the disciple-making church is maturity-oriented. Perhaps the hardest part of Paul's definition of discipleship in Philippians 2:4 is the part where he says, *look not only to your own interests, but also to the interests of others.* That's what spiritual maturity is all about—thinking about others. Immaturity means you get angry all the time when you cannot get your way; it means getting your feelings hurt because of what others say; it means always feeling that no one cares. Jesus constantly instructed his disciples in servanthood. They resisted, they protested, and they rebelled. We can expect modern-day disciples to do the same.

Maturity happens when people become intentional about spiritual growth, and this often occurs in a small group. The small group isn't the only place where disciples can grow toward maturity, but it is certainly an important one. Jesus used the small-group model. The Twelve were the original small group. Other ways to grow spiritually include personal Bible study, a daily quiet time, prayer, ministry involvement, and evangelism.

Spiritual maturity does not come easily or quickly. It is a lifelong process for followers of Jesus Christ. Don't expect instant results when you lead your church on a journey toward making disciples. There will be victories along the way, albeit small ones. Celebrate all of them. Don't be distracted or discouraged by defeats.

Normative for God's People

An emphasis on growing toward maturity will be a threat to many. It will identify their own stagnation and challenge them out of their comfortable complacency.

We need to understand that reform, revisioning, and transitioning are normative for God's people. In the Bible, God's people are always changing directions.

* From slavery in Egypt to the promised land in Canaan
* From cultural dominance in Israel to exile in Babylon
* From Pharisaism in first century Palestine to freedom in Christ
* From Judaism to Christianity
* From house church to church building
* From ecclesiastical corruption to Reformation

Every time God's people embarked on a new journey there was discontentment, heartache, suffering, and even martyrdom, but in the end there was deliverance and salvation.

Count the cost. You can bet that some people will fall away from church when the church becomes intentional about making disciples. The multitudes abandoned Jesus, and in the end it was the multitude that cried out for his Crucifixion.

Defraying the Cost

The few whom Jesus discipled became the band that turned the world upside down. Certainly, the costs are sometimes great. The rewards are even greater.

"The Blessing" is a ministry that has emerged since Mission Baptist became intentional about making disciples. Don was a marginal church member at best. He had attended regularly in the eighties then went through a bad divorce and dropped out for several years. When the train turned around, Don was one of the first to rejoin the group of passengers. He was asked to take a vital role in the music ministry, offering a new, jazzier version of music.

Don was excited about this new destination. He was also beginning to grow as a disciple. He came to me one day to talk about an idea he had for a ministry. He was asking for permission and for my blessing. His idea was to have a Christmas party for some of the needy children in the community. To get it organized, he would talk to the local Christian community ministry organization and get from them the names of children in the community who might benefit from such a ministry.

As the engineer of this train, I had been one who first planted the seeds of doubt about our old destination. It didn't take long to get a group of other malcontents to join me. But I was trained to lead the train in the old, traditional way. While fully supporting the new direction, I still had a wistful eye on the track behind us. In the beginning, I was apprehensive about my new role. In the old role, I was fully in charge of all, or at least most, of the church's ministry. If I didn't do it or have a big hand in it, it probably didn't get done. If someone came to me with an idea for what our church should be doing, it was expected that I should take the lead in getting it done.

Now my role was becoming that of a facilitator, an equipper, a resource person for ministry rather than the main minister. I was not entirely comfortable with this new role in the beginning.

When Don came to me with his idea, I had reservations. My feeling was that no one would come to the party because the children and their families would have reservations about being labeled as "needy." I expressed these feelings to Don, but I also gave my blessing and full support to him if he wanted to try. What he did with that ministry has been nothing short of remarkable.

Recognizing that he could not shoulder such a responsibility alone, he mobilized a team of folks to help him. People became excited about the idea. The first year a handful of children came. However, there were enough there to win me over from the skeptics.

The group named the party "The Blessing." It was appropriately named. The excited smiles on the faces of the children, the tears in the eyes of the parents and grandparents who came with them, the heartfelt thanks expressed to the team—all of this would insure that each year this ministry would grow. In the third year of "The Blessing," fifty-five children received gifts. Our fellowship hall could barely contain the number of people who attended. Our hearts could barely contain the joy and fullness we felt. One couple discovered that one of the needy families was related to them. They had no idea that the family had fallen on such hard times. Another young mother, weeping openly, said that next year she wanted to get on her feet so that she could be on the giving end of "The Blessing."

I am not suggesting that any other church adopt this ministry. What I am suggesting is that when a church becomes intentional about making disciples, it can be the most exciting journey imaginable.

The book of Revelation is about the coming again of Jesus. John the Revelator wrote graphically about the coming tribulation. To me, the most important verse of the whole book is found in the last chapter (22:12): *Behold, I am coming soon! My reward is with me, and I will give to everyone according to what he has done.*

Tribulation is followed by rewards for those who remain faithful. That is a great biblical promise and I think it applies to revitalizing the church. There will be no shortage of tribulation in the change process. Hear it again: *change is painful!* But we also need to hear that God blesses the faithful, and servanthood has its own rewards.

Some of the cost is defrayed by the blessings. Not all, mind you, but enough to make it worthwhile. "The Blessing" is one huge rebate at Mission. There have been others, perhaps of lesser notoriety and of varying dividends, but they have been and continue to be there nonetheless.

The Cost of Doing Nothing

There are also costs attached to doing nothing. I meet weekly with a group of pastors. We are a reading group and we are learning to be accountable to each other for our reading assignments and our faithfulness in meeting together. One of the pastors is a Methodist who has a three-point charge. One of the churches is small with only a handful attending on Sunday morning. By most criteria and measurements, they are not effective. In short, they are doing little. Yet they have tensions and church fights just like transitioning churches. Conflict comes whether a church does nothing or tries to move forward. If we will experience conflict regardless, we might as well experience it when we are trying to do the right things. Who wants a church built on weak relationships, weak accountability structures, weak worship, or weak and ineffective discipleship? I like what Steve Arterburn says about accountability: "No one has a faith that can be free from accountability to others. Lack of accountability is a clear sign of lack of faith in God and the presence of a faith in self is built on self-assertion and ego."[9]

A denominational worker friend tells a story—he swears it's true—about a church in a remote, rural part of his state. It is located in a place called Hell-Hole Swamp. They give virtually nothing to the denomination's missions program, they go years without a single conversion, and they are about as isolated as a church can get. Yet, in the past forty years they have had three church splits.

Wouldn't you think that both these churches are following the path of least resistance? Wouldn't you assume that they would be relatively free from conflict and turmoil? Of course not. I contend that the cost of doing nothing is far greater than the cost of being progressive and dreaming new dreams.

For twenty-eight years I have pastored the same church. The church has changed enormously during that time. It is possible, I think, to divide the twenty-eight years into two distinct periods. The first ten years I would call my "Pre-passion Period." This does not mean I had no enthusiasm for what I was doing. It does mean I operated in a different paradigm. My motivation was to be a good and placating pastor. I tried to do all the right things. I visited everybody in the church at least once a year those first few years. I did everything I could to shepherd the flock and keep everyone reasonably happy.

The next fifteen years in that period I refer to as the "Passion Period." I did not have a blinding-light, Damascus-road experience, but something happened to transform how I perceived my role as a pastor. I call it a passion period because I believe God gave me a passion to operate in a new paradigm. Instead of being a placating pastor, I became a visionary pastor. I still ministered to people, but their happiness wasn't my primary concern. My passion was in making disciples as Jesus commanded us. Real disciples take care of each other. The ordained clergy is still available for crisis ministry, but his/her primary focus is not in placating the people, but in casting a vision for the people to reach their full potential in the Kingdom of God.

Making disciples in this way became my passion more than a decade ago. It became the reason I got up in the mornings. In the "Pre-passion Period" I used a lot of energy offering pastoral care. I expended energy but not passion. There is a vast difference between energy and passion. Now I work out of my passion. The energy level is actually higher, and I believe it is because I am operating from my spiritual gifts.

I discovered something else along the way. During this placating-pastor, "Pre-passion Period," despite my best efforts, people occasionally still got mad and left the church. I would beat myself up every time trying to figure out why they left. These lamentations were especially draining. Sometimes people would get mad and not leave, which meant they stayed and made everybody miserable. During the "Passion Period," people would get mad and leave or sometimes they would leave without explanation. I concluded, therefore, that people will get mad and leave no matter what I do, so I should follow my calling.

I submit to you that the cost will be greater for the churches that do not change and transition to something new. In the next few years, I believe there will be basically four kinds of churches in regard to change.

(1) Churches that refuse to change. Most of these will die. They will keep their doors open for a few more years, but their eventual demise is inevitable. There are many churches in America who are one generation, or in some cases one decade, away from extinction. Hospice care will always be needed for these churches. They will need someone to hold their hand and administer last rites. Churches are like people when it comes to a death sentence. There is much denial in these churches. Ask them how things are going, and they will reply that they have never been better. Denial is one of the stages of a terminally ill patient and likewise of terminal churches.

(2) *Churches that resist change.* These churches may make cosmetic changes but put up a strong fight until they face a "change or die" ultimatum. There are resilient forces in such churches who see change as a threat to their power base. People fall away from these churches like chunks from an iceberg. Some may, in the end, learn to go along with change, but much damage will be done in the meantime. Church fights lead to brokenness.

(3) *Churches that embrace change.* These churches have worked through change with intentionality. They have said good-bye to the old and turned to embrace the new. They begin to welcome change because they see change as evidence that God is moving. *Old things have passed away; behold, all things have become new. (2 Cor 5:17 NKJV)*

(4) New churches. New church starts are on the cutting edge of change. Many of them are "unintentional" church starts. They are the chunks that have broken away because they have grown weary of churches who either refuse to change or who resist it so strongly that they drive people away.

I received a call one Sunday night recently asking if I could come to a deacons' meeting at a church in my area. This small downtown Baptist church was without a pastor and needed guidance concerning their denominational missions giving. When you're in one place for twenty-eight years, you become the village priest, and if you've done anything right in those twenty-eight years, you also become a kind of spiritual guru.

After a lengthy discussion about the primary topic on the agenda, I shared a piece of information stating that many pastors coming out of seminary would rather begin a new church than try to transition an old one. One of the deacons at the meeting is a building contractor. He drew a superb analogy when he said, "Yeah, it's much easier to build a new house than remodel an old one. I'd much rather build a new house because even after you've remodeled, you've still got an old house."

How far can we carry that analogy when it comes to transitioning a church? It is probably true that it is far easier to begin a new church than it is to take a 100-year-old church and transition it into something new and vibrant. Mission Baptist Church is a testimony to the fact that an older church can live again, but what about the second part of the contractor's analogy? Do churches that have remodeled and revisioned still have "an old house"?

I think not. In remodeling a house, one builds on the foundation. The final result, if done well, is a beautiful old house sometimes built with materials superior to what is on today's market. In addition, there are many new features added such as the modern conveniences associated with plumbing, wiring, and insulation. The basic structure in a remodeled house remains intact. The same thing can happen to the church that wisely and prudently transitions over a period of time. The "remodeling" is arduous and sometimes painful, but the end result, when done well, is a church with a solid foundation and a renewed appearance both in style and substance.

Notes

[1] Dan Southerland, *Transitioning: Leading Your Church Through Change* (Grand Rapids MI: Zondervan, 1999), 125.

[2] Barry Winders, "How to Factor Postmodernism into Your Church's Compass Heading," *Net Results* (July/August 2001), 4.

[3] Southerland, *Transitioning,* 127.

[4] N. Gordon Cosby, *By Grace Transformed* (New York: Crossroad Publishing Company, 1999), 10.

[5] Raymond Bailey, *Jesus the Preacher* (Nashville: Broadman, 1990), 59.

[6] George Bullard, "Learnings from Recent Cluster Congregational Transformation Processes," *Net Results* (February 2002), 27.

[7] Edward H. Hammett, *The Gathered and Scattered Church* (Macon GA: Smyth & Helwys, 1999), 49.

[8] Michael Yaconelli, *Messy Spirituality* (Grand Rapids MI: Zondervan, 2002), 46.

[9] Steve Arterburn, *Toxic Faith* (Nashville: Oliver Nelson, 1991), 183.

Mentaland and Spiritual Toughness

We pray for our enemies who give us reason to pray. —Samuel Freedman

My dad was a World War II veteran. He was a foot soldier and was wounded twice in Italy. He lost two brothers in the war, one in Belgium and another in the infamous Bataan Death March in the Philippines. I cannot imagine the mental toughness he needed to get through the experience of war. His generation is only now being recognized for its unique contribution to our nation's history. Tom Brokaw documented the generation's greatness in his popular book *The Greatest Generation*.

When I was about eight or nine years old, my dad took me to a war movie about the life and heroic deeds of Audie Murphy. The movie was not only about Audie Murphy, but it also starred Audie Murphy. The movie's name was *To Hell and Back*. I only remember one scene from the movie. Audie and his fellow combatants were pinned down by a machine gun nest and knew they had to do something. Audie's plan was to rush the machine gun. His rallying cry was, "Come on men, they can kill us but they can't eat us." That was mental toughness.

Somehow I always imagined my dad that way in combat. I certainly knew him to have that kind of mental toughness. Growing up, I only saw my dad cry one time. That was when his mother died, and I only saw one tear then. I never saw him cry again until he was old. Remember that those were the days before men learned that crying was not a sign of weakness and before we learned the harm of suppressing our emotions and feelings.

I played football in high school. We weren't good, but we had coaches who thought we should be. They pushed us hard. My junior varsity coach died within the past year. His name was Jerry Daniel. We called him Doc. Doc was about the toughest man I ever knew besides my dad. Doc's wife was a beautiful woman, but no one on our football team dared even look in her direction. Why? Because we knew Doc would tear us apart limb from limb.

I should have learned a lot about mental toughness because I had good teachers, but nothing prepared me for how mentally tough I would need to be to pastor a church in transition. The state level of my denomination sponsored a gathering of what they called innovative churches. Pastors and other staff members from about thirty churches were present. Most of them were pastors of new church starts. A few others, like myself, were pastors of churches in the process of transitioning from traditional to innovative.

I remember that in a dialogue session, one of the new church start pastors looked at us who were transitional pastors and said, "You are the toughest men I know." I didn't feel worthy of the compliment but understood all too well what he meant.

In his book *Managing Transitions: Making the Most of Changes,* William Bridges describes a time in transition that he calls the "neutral zone." It is the time between the old reality and the new paradigm. He lists six dangers to expect during this time (Sam Gore, an acquaintance of mine adapted these slightly to apply to church life):

(1) Anxiety rises and motivation falls. Pastors and staff already live with more anxiety than is healthy for anyone. Try telling the pastor of a traditional church that he/she needs to move the church into new paradigms. "What is one of the first things I can expect to happen?" is the question usually asked first. "Well," comes the reply, "you can expect more anxiety and less motivation."

What's the response going to be? "All right, bring on the Maalox"? I hardly think so. Most of us would run from and not toward such a scenario. Is it any wonder that church leadership shies away from radical change? Who needs more anxiety?

Yet it must be said that transitioning will produce anxiety by the ton. Therefore, a certain spiritual readiness is needed. This is why it is important to create a holy discontent in the congregation. Healthy dissatisfaction with the way things are at present gives a clear motivation to want to make things better. However, holy discontent alone is not enough. A clear vision and focus for where the church is going is also absolutely essential.

This "neutral zone" is messy. Motivation can fall simply from the weight of the transition. The "neutral zone" becomes more like a twilight zone with the church's leadership walking around like zombies at times.

(2) People in the neutral zone miss more Sundays than in other times. This should come as no surprise to anyone. When motivation suffers, it permeates the life of the whole church. Attendance at services sometimes suffers.

Let's be honest. Despite what we like to think, we play the numbers game. We pay attention to the three B's: buildings, budgets, and bodies. We have been conditioned to think that these numbers measure our success and effectiveness as a church. Many of us have been conditioned by our denomination to think that way, but we also get that message from our culture. The success on Wall Street each day is measured by the rise and fall of numbers.

One of the first things that might suffer on this journey is that people will stay away from church on Sunday morning.

Not many pastors have the mental and spiritual toughness to deal with a potential drop in numbers. It may or may not happen, but don't be surprised if it does.

(3) Old problems or weaknesses, long patched over and dealt with, may rise again in full bloom. Unfortunately, stirring the waters also stirs up other things. We have this fish bowl sitting on a little table in our breakfast nook. There is a green plant sticking out the top of the glass bowl with its roots fully exposed in the water. In the bottom are colorful plastic rocks. It came in a kit with instructions. There were instructions about feeding the fish and cleaning the water.

The cleaning job only has to be done once a week. We're supposed to take the plant out and set it aside. Then we pour about one-third of the water out of the bowl, being careful not to pour the fish out in the process. Finally, we refill the bowl with distilled water.

The first time we did this, we thought we had done something wrong. The water looked horrible. There was a whole lot of fish fecal matter floating around in the water and it took a good long while for it to settle to the bottom again and leave the water looking clear.

What we had done, of course, was stir up all the sediment from the bottom. The same thing happens in church when we stir the waters. A lot of stuff gets stirred up from the bottom that may have been suppressed for a long time.

Churches as systems have an awful propensity to suppress and even deny the existence of problems. Most pastors avoid conflict like the plague. We have strong tendencies toward suppression, denial, and avoidance of trouble and conflict. Many churches are not healthy systems in this way. They are dysfunctional, just like families.

Be prepared, church leaders. When the waters are stirred, be ready to deal with the sediment that bubbles up. Be prepared with mental and spiritual toughness.

(4) In the neutral zone, leaders are often overloaded, signals become mixed, priorities get confused, and information gets miscommunicated. Be diligent—diligent to work harder at communicating, harder at keeping priorities in order, harder at clarity.

During the transitioning period, church leaders will be overworked because they lead two churches in one—the old church and the new, emerging church. Many of the same people who made the traditional program church work will be involved in birthing something new alongside the old church. Their physical and spiritual energies will be taxed to the point of exhaustion.

It is important for the senior pastor to give extra attention to overworked leaders. They need to hear success stories of transformed lives. These stories become times of celebration. They can be told orally in three- or four-minute segments during Sunday morning worship. Another option is to present them as a page in the worship folder. You can also place the stories in a church newsletter.

Overworked leaders need to hear words of encouragement. Utilize the gifts of your laypeople. In our church, Miss Opal is an encourager. She's one of those saintly ladies who can quote more Bible verses and make the correct application of the verses better than anyone I know. People whom she has touched call her an "angel." Through the years, she wrote me scores of notes, sometimes to thank me for a sermon, sometimes to thank me for being her pastor. She is my best cheerleader and plays this role for many others.

I asked Miss Opal on more than one occasion if she would drop a note to individuals I thought needed a word of encouragement. She was always too happy to oblige. Find these cheerleaders in your congregation. Put their spiritual gifts of encouragement to use.

Church leaders need a lot of prayer during the time of transition. In addition to Miss Opal, I called on several people to pray for us during this messy transition time. Prayer is a powerful tool for toughening.

A group of our youth went on a mission trip to Memphis, Tennessee. They were involved in everything from light construction to backyard Bible clubs. Adults in the church were asked to become prayer partners with a youth. Upon their return, the youth testified that they felt empowered knowing people prayed for them back home. One young lady wrote this note to me: *Thank you so much for praying for all of us while we were gone to Memphis (Lord knows we needed it!). The trip was definitely an experience for me. I was forced to step out of my "comfort zone" on several occasions. Getting on the roof was one of them. If I didn't know that I had prayer and support from people like you at home, I don't know that I would have been able to do it.*

Enlist people who will do nothing but pray. Ask malcontents to pray. Call the entire church to prayer. On more than one occasion, usually for special events, we had prayer vigils at the church. During a twelve- or twenty-four-hour period, we ask someone to be at the church constantly for prayer, coming in twenty- or thirty-minute intervals. Don't underestimate the power of prayer to give the mental and spiritual toughness needed for transitioning.

(5) Given ambiguities of the neutral zone, people may become polarized between those who want to rush forward and those who want to go back to the old ways. Discord arises. The quintessential neutral zone in the Bible is the wilderness wandering after the exodus. The freed Hebrew people were fine for a while—a short while. Soon they began to murmur. When they grew tired of the manna that God so graciously provided for them, many of them longed for the fleshpots of Egypt. At least in Egypt they had meaty stew on occasion instead of the same old manna.

The presence of disgruntled and murmuring church people requires mental toughness. All discontent will not be holy. Some of it will be nasty and vicious. Some people will be bulldog-tenacious in wanting to hold on to the past.

Loren Mead, head of the Alban Institute, spoke before a group of Baptists in North Carolina and gave what he called "Twelve Rules for White Water Rafting."[1] These rules have enormous implications for a church in transition.

1. Don't complain about the whiter water. That's what you came for. Enjoy it! Don't complain that you're not in a sailboat.
2. Decide before you start whether you're going to steer from the front or the back. Either one will work, but you've got to be clear and sure before you start.
3. Someone needs to call the orders clearly.
4. Rest when you come to a calm place because it's not going to last for long.
5. Never stop paddling even if it seems hopeless.
6. If you get into trouble, don't panic. (Assuming that you'll probably get in trouble.)
7. Don't be surprised if the boat doesn't go where you want it to.
8. On a raft, the more activity there is on the right, the more the raft goes left. The more activity there is on the left, the more it goes to the right.
9. If you go under, let go of everything; eventually you'll come back up.
10. Everyone paddles furiously to get somewhere, but it's really the current that will take you downstream.
11. Trust the raft and stay in it. It's the safest way to get through white water.
12. Remember that the people in the raft are the ones who will pull you out of the water if you fall. They are also the ones you must eat supper with.

(6) Churches become vulnerable to attacks from Satan. When are we most vulnerable to Satan's attacks? What weakens us to them? Anxiety, apathy, lagging attendance, problems upon problems, overwork, miscommunication, polarization, and discord all make us weak. These issues signal a vulnerability problem.

Many people call this vulnerability spiritual warfare. The forces of evil are alive and well in our day, and you can be sure that they will not sit still and silent when the church is on the move. Paul understood this in his letter to the Ephesians. In chapter 6, he admonishes them to put on the full armor of God for the battles that will come. Spiritual warfare calls for spiritual weapons. Paul listed a number of them:

Gird your loins with truth. There are non-negotiable aspects of the faith. It is important that each church decide which truths are non-negotiable. These truths are called core beliefs. We don't need to debate them for a long time. The church must stand for something, and that something is the gospel truth. Deciding on a core set of beliefs is a great weapon against untruth.

At Mission, we assumed we knew what we believed and that the average person in the pew would also know. Once a church begins to open its heart to the moving of the Holy Spirit and its doors to all kinds of people, many people sitting in the pews will know little about the church except what they have personally experienced about the grace of God. That's a good start in their belief system, but it becomes essential for the church at this point to document its core belief system in writing.

Put on the breastplate of righteousness. God's people are called to be righteous and holy. A breastplate protects the most vulnerable part of one's body—the heart. Christians must lead exemplary lives in this day of compromise and promiscuity. I am not advocating elitism or a "holier-than-thou" attitude. One value that needs to be taught repeatedly in various church settings is the value of righteousness. It is indispensable as a weapon against all manner of evil.

Shod your feet with the equipment of the gospel of peace. Peace is often elusive when a church is re-visioning and transitioning. Some people do not want to make significant changes, and they have difficulty finding peace. Some push too hard for change, and peace eludes them. The pastor and other leaders must walk a fine line. Change that disrupts the fellowship and new ideas that erupt into open conflict are not the end results anyone wants. Great wisdom is needed at this point. Shodding one's feet with the gospel of peace enables the church to walk in unity if not harmony, in love if not conformity.

Take the shield of faith. In Daniel 3, Shadrach, Meshach, and Abednego face the fiery furnace with great faith, saying, "O Nebuchadnezzar, we do not need to defend ourselves to you. If we are thrown into the blazing furnace, the God whom we serve is able to save us" (3:16-17 NLT). Not all fires of transitioning will be as hot as the one faced by the three Hebrews who stood before King Nebuchadnezzar. Some fires will be more like a sauna, uncomfortable while you're in it, but refreshing and cleansing when you're finished. Regardless of the heat index and the benefits on the other side, fires can be uncomfortable. Don't ever try to enter a fire without great faith. Shadrach, Meshach, and Abednego were passionate and committed to what they were doing. Tom Bandy said that such great faith is required to transition a church that the pastor must be willing to give up the parsonage and the pension. That is serious faith. Without that kind of strong protection, the flaming arrows will penetrate a shield made of lesser material.

Take the helmet of salvation. Mental toughness, forged in the same fire as the strong faith, will deflect many weapons in the spiritual warfare brought on by transitioning. Salvation happens through grace, not through our abilities or cleverness or goodness. The helmet of salvation protects us from the fallacy of trying to save ourselves. Total dependence on God is the way to salvation. It is the only way through the battles that rage around revitalizing a church.

Take the sword of the Spirit, which is the Word of God. A sword is both an offensive weapon and a defensive weapon. God's Word has appropriate insight for every battle and every circumstance. It would be disastrous for church leadership to attempt to move the church forward through any process of re-visioning without being armed with God's Word. One of the best ways to read and study the Bible for this process is to try to allow the Bible story to become our story.

Luke 24 offers an example in the Emmaus Road story. Two disciples walked away from Jerusalem. They probably felt betrayed by the religious institutions who conspired to kill Jesus. They were confused by the events of the past few days, and reports of a resurrection only added to their state of confusion. Jesus, unrecognizable at first, came and walked beside them. He gave understanding to them and helped them make sense of the turmoil. This incident provides a great metaphor for the church! We are called to walk beside the hurting and betrayed of our day and to help them make sense of their confusion and chaos. Many times the religious establishment—the church—has hurt them. In this way, Jesus' story becomes our story. Twenty centuries of time may divide the original incident from our modern experience, but the application eradicates factor of time. We become the church that drives people away from God. Our call is to walk beside those who are fleeing and help them make sense of what has happened. We should offer them only Jesus and sweet fellowship, not an institution.

A close look at any of the dangers of transitioning is enough to make a pastor and/or staff member shudder. Are we ready to deal with it? Not unless we are prepared with the whole armor of God.

I don't mean to sound timid, but one of the most obvious ways to move forward is to make small changes to minimize the dangers of transitioning. Give the church culture time to absorb small changes, celebrate small victories widely and loudly, and then move on to the next step.

A new pastor moved into our area a few years ago. We became friends right away and went to lunch together a few times. He was intrigued by some of the changes we had implemented in our church. He wanted to do the same things in his church, which at the time was traditional and resistant to change. I cautioned him about not going too fast. He didn't listen, and he didn't last. He was gone in a few months, consumed by the fiery flames of resistance.

I'm convinced that we don't celebrate enough in churches. Every week in our worship folder, we highlight victories. We once listed what we called the "Vital Signs" of the week, which, as you might guess, consisted of the attendance and offering figures from the previous week. That sent a clear signal to everyone in attendance that we valued the three B's (bodies, bucks, and buildings).

Several years ago, we began to highlight what we now consider to be the real "vital signs" of the church. Every week we publish two or three blurbs about a ministry that has taken place in the life of the church. Some are confidential and can't be publicized; for instance, we can't publicize the fact that one of our deacons did impromptu marriage counseling with a couple that probably saved their marriage. The reasons are obvious. However, we can put in print that one of our small groups is going on a regular basis to the new Hispanic church in the area to help with the children's program. Celebrate little changes with fanfare. The message is sent over and over, week after week, that the church's real vital signs are not numbers but changed lives.

Our denomination has something called an Annual Church Profile (ACP). It asks for every statistic imaginable:

- the number of baptisms
- the number of people in the music program
- the number of people in short-term discipleship
- the number of people in ongoing discipleship
- the total financial receipts
- the money given to missions
- the money spent for literature
- the value of church property

A church in transition needs to celebrate something besides the three B's. The B's are easy to measure, easy to calculate, and at the end of the day when all the totals are added up, churches can look back and say, "You know, we're making progress. We have grown by 3.7 percent over the past fourteen years. Brother, let's keep on preaching the Word. We must be doing something right." The real "vital signs" are difficult to measure because they are in story form. Forget the statistics. Tell the stories. Celebrate the victories.

Doing battle and seeing victory adds to the mental toughness. The little engine that could made it to the top of the hill because she refused to give in to her fatigue and dwindling energies. She was mentally tough.

They that go down to the sea in ships do business in great waters. These see the works of the Lord and His wonders in the deep (Psalm 107:23-24). Numerous phobias plague people, but one of the most common is hydrophobia, the fear of water. Water can be a frightening thing, especially deep and dark water. After all, we have to use a different skill to stay afloat in water than we do to maneuver on dry land. It's called swimming, but no one can swim forever so the water can be a much more dangerous place than dry land.

The psalmist says, *Those who go down to the sea in ships, Who do business on great waters; They have seen the works of the LORD, And His wonders in the deep (Psalm 107:23-24, NASB).* God is always calling us to a deeper walk with him, a deeper commitment, a deeper faith. He is calling us to GO DEEP. Therefore, the sailboat is a symbol of God calling us to do business in deep waters.

We knew God was calling us to deep financial waters. In early 2002, we began a three-phased, multi-million-dollar building program. Where will we get all the money? None of us has a clue, but we believe God knows and he will help us find it. That is what it means to go deep.

Many of the people in any congregation do business in deep waters financially every day. It isn't always within the church, but daily many of those in the congregation are in contact with business people who have their finger on a lot of wealth. We asked them to be ready to tell the church's story to anyone at the first opportunity and how we are moving out into deep financial waters.

God is also calling us to deep spiritual waters. Over the past few years we have been known in our area for doing church a little bit differently. We have different worship; we do Sunday school differently; we offer small Bible study groups. All of that is good, but the most important thing is that we are known as a church that moves in deep spiritual waters. Unless we are going deep spiritually in our individual lives,

- our worship will degenerate into performance and entertainment, lacking a genuine experience with God.
- our Bible study will degenerate into intellectual discussions, lacking spiritual wisdom.
- our ministries will degenerate into social programs, lacking compassion.

We stand on the authority of the deep waters of the Bible. We have no other authority. We should not teach any Sunday school lesson, sing any hymn or praise song as a soloist or as a congregation, have any discussion on a social issue, or even give a cup of cold water unless we do it under the authority of God's Word.

Our logo is designed to remind all of us, especially those who lead, that our call is to deep spiritual waters. It should remind those who lead in Bible study, those who sing or play an instrument in our music ministry, those who lead small groups, those who are involved in any ministry, that unless they are moving into deep spiritual waters they should not be leading.

How can we sing about amazing grace if we aren't experiencing it daily? How can we teach the Bible if its Word is not hidden in our hearts? How can we lead someone to Christ if we do not have an intimate relationship with him ourselves?

There is something else about a sailboat portrayed in full sail. It implies that we are on a journey. There is no reason to unfurl the sails unless we are going somewhere. The logo is designed to keep us constantly asking the question, are we on a journey? The church will never journey farther than its collective members. If the individual members aren't growing, then the church isn't growing. Following Christ is a spiritual journey. The church will never travel far if the individual followers aren't going anywhere.

Finally, the sailboat does not have power of its own. It depends on the wind. That wind for the church is the Holy Spirit. Like the wind, the Holy Spirit is an invisible force that moves us out into the deep and sometimes treacherous water.

We are beginning to talk about things like membership requirements. We want to send the message that we take seriously the call to deep spiritual waters. In effect, we would say to newcomers, "If you are not willing to go deep, this is not your church." I agree with those who predict that the "membership" as we have known it will probably need to cease to exist for the church who wants to sail into deep spiritual waters. Church membership in the old paradigm is all about privilege—the privilege of being able to buy a plot in the cemetery or the privilege of being able to use the facilities without charge for our sons and daughters to get married. "Membership" for the church moving in deep spiritual waters will need to revolve around growth into Christian discipleship. It will probably not be called membership at all since that term denotes privilege. I am a member of a fitness center. That membership gives me the privilege of being able to use thousands of dollars worth of expensive exercise equipment. Did God ever intend for membership in his body to mean privilege? I don't think so.

Some churches have already moved in that direction, but we are only beginning to talk about it. We don't know what it might look like in its final form, but one of our goals should be that everyone around us would know without any doubt that Mission Baptist Church is moving in deep spiritual waters.

God is calling us to deep evangelistic waters. *Evangelism* is a word that carries a lot of baggage. We have seen too many televangelists with slick polyester suits and bad hairpieces to know what evangelism truly is. Evangelism is the sharing of the gospel in the power of the Holy Spirit with the purpose of leading someone to a saving knowledge of Jesus Christ. Jesus offers eternal life with God and all their loved ones who have gone before them. The stakes are high in evangelism. The waters are deep. Every time we see this symbol in our church—the boat—we are reminded that the eternity of souls is at stake in deep waters.

Then, there is our slogan: "A Church That Cares." Do we dare to say that? That's definitely treading into deep waters. Our slogan holds us accountable to be what we say we are. There are voices that call to us from the deep about that one:

• Don't say it unless you mean it.
• Don't adopt it as a slogan unless you can back it up with your actions.
• Care for all people. You can't say you care for some people and not care about others. That means you have to care as much about the body-

79

pierced, tattooed Gen-Xer who has never been to church as you do about the middle-aged man or woman who has been in church all his or her life.

• Do you really care about the "least of these" that Jesus spoke about?

Deep waters are indeed frightening and forbidding. It is much safer in the shallow water. You never hear about a ship sinking in dry dock. Remember, our Savior is the Master of the Sea. Acts 1:8 says the Holy Spirit came upon the early disciples and told them to go into Jerusalem (their own hometown), into Judea (the region around them), into Samaria (the foreign neighbors), and to the uttermost parts of the world. Deep waters, yes. But in those deep waters we find the greatness and the wonder of God.

Note

[1] Loren Mead, "Leading the Church into the Future," audiocassette produced by the Laity Leadership Team of the Baptist State Convention of North Carolina, Cary NC, 1999.

The Prophet

The light shines in the darkness, but the darkness has not understood it. There came a man who was sent from God; his name was John. He came as a witness to testify concerning that light, so that through him all men might believe. He himself was not the light; he came only as a witness to the light. They asked him, "Then who are you? Are you Elijah?" He said, "I am not." "Are you the Prophet?" He answered, "No." Finally they said, "Who are you? Give us an answer to take back to those who sent us. What do you say about yourself?" John replied in the words of Isaiah the prophet, "I am the voice of one calling in the desert, Make straight the way for the Lord." (John 1:5-8, 21-23 NIV)

Alan Roxborough makes the point that the pastor cannot be the prophet.[1] Instead, the pastor is the poet. The prophet's role is to speak prose and stir the waters. The pastor's role is to interpret the movement of the waters.

Jesus said that a prophet does not have honor in his own country. I have found this to be true for a variety of reasons. The pastor who has sat by the bedside of the dying, blessed the newborns, married the young, and walked with parishioners through the dark valleys will find it difficult to exchange the pastor's hat for the prophet's hat.

This is perhaps unfortunate since the pastor knows the congregation better than anyone. Apathy is rampant in the stagnant church. Apathy may be the single greatest hindrance to a vibrant and dynamic church. The pastor watches with a heavy heart as members slip into the throes of apathy. The pastor hears the parishioner say, "I'd like to buy twenty dollars' worth of God—not enough to get me too excited or keep me up nights, just enough to make me feel good about myself."[2] Such attitudes drain the life out of a pastor. Is the pastor powerless to do anything about it? Can he/she speak a prophetic voice to stirs stagnant waters?

That a vast majority of churches in America are plateaued or declining is well documented. Why would congregations not welcome the pastor taking on the prophetic role in order to turn the church around? The truth is that turning a church around and making it vibrant and growing again is a threat to many congregants. Bill Easum has noted that the more pastors get involved in transitioning a church, the more opposition and hostility they experience. The hostility comes not only from the congregation but sometimes from the denomination as well.[3]

This hostility to change has resulted in a grave ministerial crisis throughout North America. It helps account for several emerging trends:

- A dramatic increase in the number of forced terminations in the pastorate.
- An increase in the number of ordained clergy who leave the pastorate for other lines of work.
- A rash of early retirements by pastors.
- An increase in the number of independent, nondenominational churches as pastors bypass the bureaucracy and maze of denominational institutions.
- Many other pastors become resigned to laboring in a dying church, resulting in an epidemic of psychological and emotional depression.
- An apparent all-time high in the number of clergy who suffer from addictions of one kind or another.[4]

The pastor or staff member is not completely powerless, but the prophetic role is limited because of some of the factors noted above. I know of a pastor in a nearby community who clashed with the church's leadership over a matter that involved a drastic change in the direction of the church. He had been the pastor for twelve years. On this particular occasion, he overstepped his bounds. One Sunday after a tense business meeting in which his leadership was called into question, the church called for a "confidence" vote. His job was on the line. He barely survived the vote. Angered at being subjected to this humility, he lost his cool and snapped to the congregation, "I ought to jerk the leg off this communion table and beat the hell out of some deacons." Now imagine that pastor being called to the bedside of someone in the congregation in intensive care the next week. The comforting, pastoral role would have been strained at best, impossible at worst.

I am not suggesting that the above example was in any way the work of an authentic prophet of God. Actually, it sounds as if this particular pastor had allowed the Enemy to control his emotions at that point. His actions were indicative, I think, of the enormous pressures clergy feel when they dare to attempt to move the church in a different direction.

It is not likely that even the outside prophet could have gotten away with the above retort, but it would have been more easily dismissed. "At least we won't have to put up with him again," the congregation would say.

I saw a cartoon in a religious publication in which a pastor stood in front of the church's attendance board in a church corridor. The board read, "Membership 863, Sun. attendance 610, Overnight Change in Pastor's Approval Rating—2%."[5] I am not suggesting the pastor needs to be concerned about approval ratings. The pastor is not in a popularity contest. However, the pastor or any other staff member needs to understand that his/her role involves earning an entry into the lives of people. This is essential for pastoral care or visionary leadership.

Am I a harp that the hand of the mighty may touch me, or a flute that his breath may pass through me?

A seeker of silences am I, and what treasure have I found in silences that I may dispense with confidence?

If this is my day of harvest, in what fields have I sowed the seed, and in what unremembered seasons?

If this indeed be the hour in which I lift up my lantern, it is not my flame that shall burn therein.

Empty and dark shall I raise my lantern,

And the guardian of the night shall fill it with oil and he shall light it also.

These things he said in words. But much in his heart remained unsaid. For he himself could not speak his deeper secret.

You have walked among us a spirit, and your shadow has been a light upon our faces.

Then said Almitra, Speak to us of Love.

And he raised his head and looked upon the people and there fell a stillness upon them. And with a great voice he said:

When love beckons to you, follow him,

Though the sword hidden among his pinions may wound you.

And when he speaks to you believe in him,

Though his voice may shatter your dreams as the north wind lays waste the garden.[6]

Making the Truth Loom Large

Walter Brueggemann speaks of the necessity of someone taking on the role to make the "truth loom large" to God's people. When that happens, the "world is set loose toward healing."[7] The authentic prophet's role is not that of a naysayer or prophet of doom. The main role of the prophet is to offer hope—the hope of renewal and revitalization. The true prophet of God comes to build up and not to tear down.

The role of the prophet is to bring God's fountain of living water to a dry and thirsty land. Listen to a prophet from the eighth century BC: *For I will pour water on the thirsty land, and streams on the dry ground; I will pour my spirit upon your descendants, and my blessings on your offspring* (Isa 44:3). This followed on the heels of a declaration in Isaiah 41:9 that *You are my servant, I have chosen you and not cast you off.*

Use this as a test for anyone who would come as an authentic prophet of God: Does the prophet have a word of hope? Church consultants tell us that a church as a living organism has a life cycle from birth to death.

However, they also say that a church doesn't have to die. It can revitalize at any point in the life cycle. The key is to set in motion forces that will begin the process of revitalization. This is what we are transitioning—a church that is dead or dying to one that has new life and new vitality. Again, Brueggemann hits it squarely on the head when he says, "Now, however, there is disclosed a new word, a new hope, a new verb, a new conversation, a new risk, a new possibility."[8] Pray fervently for a prophet or for several prophets who can bring hope in the form of a fresh word from the Lord.

The Outside Prophet

Several years ago, a Sunday-morning Ziggy cartoon showed a single frame. Ziggy stood outside looking across a beautiful landscape toward a gorgeous horizon with the sun just beginning to set. The artist did a splendid job of painting the full glory of nature. The caption from Ziggy's mouth read, "Not all realities are harsh."

The prophet brought in from the outside can speak harsh realities. He/she can analyze and scrutinize and verbalize his/her findings to the congregation. Sure, the words may fall on deaf ears, but at least the trumpet will sound.

The prophet can then be quoted and referenced for weeks and even months after his/her appearing. The beating of the prophet's drum resonates much better to most congregations than the constant pounding of the pastor's mantra.

Why is this true? For one thing, the prophet is "not one of us." His/her detachment gives instant credibility. The old saying that an expert is someone who lives more than a hundred miles away holds true. The congregation will endure the tirades of the outside prophet because they don't have to listen to him/her week after week, year after year. The prophet will disappear with the setting sun. However, he/she will leave a distinct mark. The words spoken will never be forgotten, especially if the pastor/poet is wise enough to keep the prophet's vision alive.

Moses played that role for the children of Israel. He had been gone from Egypt for forty years. He was never truly one of the Hebrews because he was raised by the Egyptian royal family. That, plus the fact that he lived on the backside of the desert for forty years, qualified him as an outsider. Outsiders enjoy a credibility that insiders can only dream about. However, the outside prophet will not enjoy instant credibility very long unless he/she has something worthwhile and hopeful to say. After the initial contact, even outside prophets have to earn credibility.

Imagine where Israel would have wound up if the classical Old Testament prophets like Jeremiah, Isaiah, Ezekiel, Amos, and Hosea had kept silent. In the New Testament era, John the Baptist's poignant preaching paved the way for another who was to come. Jesus was the poet, the one who interpreted the dance, the one who made God real to the masses. John the Baptist spoke the harsh realities of prose. The contrast in John and Jesus is remarkable. John was an ascetic who railed against the unrighteousness of his day. Jesus was more compassionate. He healed the sick and made the blind see. The crowds flocked to see and hear him. The point is that both the poet and the prose artist have their places at different times in the life of a church.

Prophets Among Us

One of our early prophets was Eddie Hammett, who has since become an author of some renown. His books published to date include *Converting the Church for the Twenty-first Century*, *The Gathered and Scattered Church*, and *Reframing Spiritual Formation*, all published by Smyth & Helwys. These books have been widely used as "prophets in paperback" to help stir the waters in a growing number of churches in North America, including our own.

As of this writing, Eddie is a consultant for the Baptist State Convention of North Carolina. We first met him in 1990 at a deacon conference conducted by our state convention. He began to sow the seeds of discontent in us at that time. A couple of years later, we brought Eddie in to lead a leadership retreat. He continued to stir the waters.

Eddie has dared to ask the hard questions. At the retreat, one lady, who was a relative newcomer to our congregation, made the statement that our church was a friendly congregation but that in the three years that she had been attending, she had experienced difficulty feeling accepted. When Eddie asked her what she meant by that, she stated that she attended without her husband and always had trouble fitting in. She also stated that she felt like an outsider since she had not grown up in the church. When Eddie pressed her further, she backed off almost apologetically, but Eddie would not let the issue rest. He pressed her for further clarification and then challenged the group to understand why this lady felt unaccepted. Only an outside prophet could have done what he did that night—and lived to tell about it!

We encourage and provide budget funds for lay leaders to attend conferences where modern-day prophets are speaking. I took our five-person staff and a lay leader to one of the conferences done by Bill Easum and Tom Bandy. Those two guys hear the beat of a distant ecclesiastical drummer.

They blew our doors off. The staff loved it. The lay leader was shell-shocked. Perhaps even more shocking to the lay leader, a conservative, old-paradigm, modernist thinker, was the fact that he knew that I loved and agreed with much of what Easum and Bandy were saying. He dropped out of church soon after that, telling someone, "I don't like the way they're doing church anymore."

More recently, I took seven leaders to an Easum/Bandy conference. They all had to take the day off work to attend. Easum and Bandy were again at their best. This group was not quite as shell-shocked. For the most part, they ate it up. The following Saturday morning they met at 7:30 for coffee to debrief what they had seen and heard.

Prophets are seldom popular with everyone. Many of the biblical prophets died for their stance against indifference, idolatry, and injustice. John the Baptist was beheaded. He would definitely have said, "It isn't easy being me." It isn't easy being a prophet in any age.

The Poet Has a Tough Job Too

Trust is an important attribute in leaders who would move a church forward in transitioning. By the time it became obvious at Mission that our deliverance from institutional enslavement was nigh, I had long since lost hope of performing the "outside prophet" role. As their pastor for fifteen years, I had become one of them. They looked to me for guidance, direction, and perhaps even protection, but my ability to stir them up with fiery diatribes had long since evaporated.

The wise pastor, I think, understands this. A friend of mine described walking out one Sunday morning after the service to greet the worshipers at the door. He had preached a prophetic sermon that Sunday on the subject of tithing and stewardship. He recalls looking at the familiar faces of his congregation as he walked out via the center aisle. "I realized that at that moment, I was not one of them. My rather scathing sermon had created a wall." Such is the plight of the prophet. A pastor has only so many of those prophetic chips to play.

I came to understand that my role as a prophet was limited. That was best left to outsiders, someone to come in and tell the truth in love. Pastors are programmed, it seems, to skirt the truth. We are the court priests, and our calling or hiring has too often been to placate the crowds, not stir them. I did some serious soul-searching to try to figure out my role. Was I the prophet or the priest? Was I the poet or the prose artist? I had been at the church at that time for more than fifteen years. Why, after so long, did I suddenly have to wrestle with my role? I'll tell you why. It takes a different set of skills to reform the church than it does to be the placating pastor. The question was whether or not I was willing to make a commitment to stay with them for as long as it took to reform. This was no easy struggle.

As outside prophets were brought in to the life of our congregation, my role became to interpret their sometimes harsh prose. That isn't always easy either. Poets can quickly become unpopular as soon as the audience starts to figure out that they are not merely interpreting but also sharing from their hearts. Prophets and poets alike can be stoned.

It bears repeating here that conflict is inevitable in the transitioning congregation. The pastor and staff must be the spiritual leaders in the conflicted church. This job may not be quite as impossible if the pastor and/or staff have not been the ones to do all the stirring of the waters. Attacks will come in any event. The pastor will not have the luxury of taking such attacks personally, even though they will sound personal at times.

Walter Brueggemann speaks of an encounter with God who is both "shockingly gracious" and "stunningly sovereign." He goes on to say, "the risk is too great, the discomfort so demanding. We much prefer to settle for a less demanding, less overwhelming meeting. Yet we are haunted by the awareness that only this overwhelming meeting [with God] gives life."[9]

The prophet does bring us into an encounter with the God who is demanding and overwhelming. It is no wonder then that people shrink from this encounter. God is not like us. He stirs us out of our comfort zone. He snaps us out of our complacency. People say they want that, but their actions say otherwise. Prophets are stoned. Priests and pastors who try to be prophets are stoned. The pastor who tries to be the prophet too often will be stoned too often and rendered ineffective and powerless to bring about transformation. Jesus said it best when he stated (sadly, I'm guessing) that the prophet may find honor everywhere but in his own country or locale.

Encounters with the living God who happens to be demanding and overwhelming also bring life. Such encounters bring reviving, reforming, revitalizing, transforming life. The prophet, then, becomes absolutely essential to the church in transition. Prophets stir passion and stimulate vision, without which there will be no transformation of God's people, no healing for the hurts of the body of Christ.

Piercing Prose

The piercing prose of prophets often stabs at the heart of the preacher as well as the parishioners. Eddie Hammett has become our prophet of choice. We have used him as a guest speaker and conference leader, and we have used his books to keep the waters moving. As he has become almost too familiar, we have looked elsewhere for a new face. God is always raising up prophets, voices crying in the wilderness, preparing the way of the Lord and church renewal.

Prophets are indispensable to transitioning. In the largely bygone days of church revival meetings, the visiting evangelists (often pastors from other churches in other locales) would be invited to come in and preach a series of sermons. Some of them were evangelistic in nature but more often, especially in later years, they became "in-church" revivals. The principle was the same as the outside prophet's role for the transitioning church. The outside prophet comes in and sets the table and perhaps even suggests the menu. After he/she leaves, it is up to the pastor, staff, and other church leaders to prepare the complete meal from appetizer, salad, entrée, beverage, and dessert.

The Support Group as Prophet

I've already noted the role of the pastoral support group through various stages of our transitioning process.

Getting a group of like-minded pastors and/or staffers together is not as easy as it sounds. Currently I meet with a group of six pastors, including myself. We have been meeting for about three years, and during that time we have invited at least a dozen more pastors in the area to join us. Our stated purpose is to read a book and then get together weekly to discuss it. We read one chapter a week. Many of our books are about church reform. For example, we have read *Growing Spiritual Redwoods* by Tom Bandy and Bill Easum, *Who Moved My Cheese?* by Spencer Johnson, and *The Divine Conspiracy* by Dallas Willard. These "paperback prophets" have stretched us out of our comfort zones. That, coupled with lively group discussions about the reading material, has been a powerful source of stimulation and encouragement for all of us.

Guided reading and church reform do not seem to be on the agendas of most pastors. Either they perceive themselves as too busy, or they have no interest in reading. One pastor nearing retirement told me that reading about cutting edge issues was not something he was interested in at this state in his career. We wonder why churches are dying.

I am currently also part of a "Learning Community for Transitioning Pastors" that meets every few weeks. We are a group of pastors involved in leading churches through transitioning, and we meet to discuss issues that are common to our situations. The group draws from a wide geographic region in North and South Carolina. Some drive more than two hours one way to get to our meetings. Our old prophet friend Eddie Hammett facilitates these sessions. Our discussions, which last for several hours including lunch, center on such issues as maintenance vs. mission, power structures in the church, keeping the vision alive, getting unstuck, and unfreezing old paradigms. We offer encouragement and support to each other, which is desperately needed. At any meeting, one or more of us are often in crisis. We recently offered support to one of our number, a pastor, who was fired for his efforts to reform and transform an old-paradigm congregation.

Early in 2002 I gathered another group of pastors in transitioning churches together in a learning community that I facilitate. One thing I discovered quite early is that all churches will go through transitioning in varying degrees of struggle, in varying stages, and with varying results. Mutual support through the struggles is helpful regardless of the situation.

The Biblical Prophets

Walter Brueggemann spoke eloquently about the role of the biblical prophets when he wrote, "The gift of freedom was taken over by the yearning for order. The human agenda of justice was utilized for security. The God of freedom and justice was co-opted for an eternal now. And in place of passion comes satiation."[10] Is there hope for the institutional church? Some would argue that all institutions are inherently evil and therefore hopeless. I have little time for such arguments. I have been given an institution called the church. I feel strongly that I have also been given a calling to reform that institution. Brueggemann was right. Religious institutions do rob Jesus' disciples of freedom. They perpetuate injustice. They subdue passion.

Enter the prophet to stir the waters, sow the seeds of discontent, disestablish the establishment, de-institutionalize the institution. Enter the prophet to renew and restore passion, call the people to celebrate what God is doing, and exorcise the demons of control, order, and security.

Notes

[1] Alan Roxborough, speaking at the Leadership Institute of the Cooperative Baptist Fellowship, Orlando FL, 27 June 2000.

[2] James Emery White, *A Search for the Spiritual: Exploring Real Christianity* (Grand Rapids MI: Baker Books, 1998). 19.

[3] Bill Easum, "How to Address the Stress Points in Turnaround Churches," *Net Results* (June 2001), 20.

[4] Ibid.

[5] *Leadership: A Practical Journal for Church Leaders* (spring 2001), 44.

[6] Kahil Gibran, *The Prophet* (New York: Alfred A. Knoff, Inc., 1973), 7, 8, 11.

[7] Walter Bruggemann, *Finally Comes the Poet* (Minneapolis: Fortress, 1989), 11.

[8] Ibid, 10.

[9] Ibid, 45.

[10] Walter Brueggeman, *The Prophetic Imagination* (Philadelphia: Fortress, 1978), 40-41.

Changing Values Before
Changing Structure

"Change values before changing structures." I first heard of this principle from Bob Gilliam, cofounder of T-Net International. I wish I had learned it a long time ago.

In seminary I received a good theological education. It grounded me solidly in the faith, gave me the tools to use in sermon preparation, and taught me skills I would need to do church in a church culture. However, there were several deficiencies in my seminary education. One of them was how to introduce change and implement change into a congregation who worshiped at the altar of "we never did it that way before." I would call my first twelve years at Mission a wilderness experience. I was not a leader; I was a wilderness wanderer. I was a good pastor, a good father, and a fairly decent human being. I was not a leader of God's people and knew nothing about how to implement change without becoming a martyr or splitting the church. As I mentioned in chapter 4, one of the few valuable things I learned in seminary about church administration was from the professor who warned us, "If you are going to become a martyr, make sure it's over something worth dying for." His words were wise for a play-it-safe church culture. They were certainly not all I needed to provide leadership to a group of people who called themselves the church in what was to become a rapidly changing, unchurched culture. Armed only with that advice in my arsenal, I figured there wasn't much worth fighting for except salvation itself, and Jesus had already done that one well.

Jesus was a change agent. He took a band of ignorant fishermen, tax collectors, and a few religious misfits and molded them into a force that would change the course of human history. He started by changing values. At his first public appearance recorded in the Gospels, he stood up to read a passage from Isaiah. After reading the passage, he dropped a bombshell. "Today," he said, "this scripture is fulfilled in your hearing" (Luke 4).

It was enough to get the synagogue leaders all riled up, and they sought to throw him down a cliff, but Jesus, knowing it was not his time yet, vanished from the crowd and went on his way. It was not time for Jesus to become a martyr. However, he had begun his work of changing values. His followers heard this new way of reading the Scriptures, and they would hear it many more times. The religious authorities would hear it again, and their fury would grow more intense each time. Three years later Jesus had so upset the religious establishment that they could not tolerate him any longer. The disciples, however, had heard enough to found a new religion called Christianity.

Jesus didn't try to upend the religious institutions of his day by working within the system for institutional reform. Instead, he invested three years of his time in the lives of a group of people. He changed their values, and then the structures were changed. A couple of decades passed before the Apostle Paul emerged on the ecclesiastical scene to give structure to the new entity called the church.

The Mission

The value that Jesus, the disciples, Paul, and others changed was the way the people of God perceived their mission. Much has been written in recent years about the mission of the church. Mike Regele, author of *The Death of the Church,* says that churches need to change the way they perceive their mission. There must first be a fundamental change in values in several areas. Let's look at four areas identified by Regele.[1]

(1) The church must change its role from being the caretaker of the parish to being a mission outpost. Within a short time of my pastorate at Mission, there was no doubt about my pastoral role and function. I was the hired hand whom the church had employed to be the village priest. I was to visit the sick, bless the babies, marry the betrothed, bury the dead, counsel the troubled, and rein in the wicked. These were my duties in the parish. That

doesn't even count preaching two or three different sermons a week, doing special Bible studies when needed or even when not.

I will always remember the Sunday that nearly sent me over the edge. It was about three minutes before 11:00. I was a few feet from the door of the hallowed sanctuary. A few more steps and I would have had my hand on the doorknob, ready to pull open the door to a congregation who waited for me to feed them for another week. Suddenly a near-hysterical woman (name withheld) in a choir robe came running up to me. Her face communicated one thing: CRISIS. I had seen that look many times before. I was once called away with the news that a choir member's mother had died that morning and we needed to get word to her before the service. So there I stood, braced and ready to hear what awful tragedy had stuck. "Preacher, preacher, the commode in the women's bathroom is running over!"

I calmly walked out to where the ushers were, took one of them aside, and told him of the crisis. Why she had chosen to tell me at that moment was not hard to figure out at all. I was, after all, the holy handyman.

A table needs moving from one building to another. The church van needs gassing up. Someone's kid gets beaten up by the churchyard bully. It's the middle of the night and a drunken husband is on the rampage. The local PTA needs a fund-raiser. A marginal church member's third cousin twice removed is in the hospital. It's another job for "holy handyman."

Churches need to be cared for. The people need caretakers. They need holy handymen and holy handywomen. I developed considerable skills in the area. I had the spiritual gift of mercy. But was this my calling?

There was a time in my ministry when I knew something was wrong. I needed to change. That was evident. First, the church would have to change their perception of my role as the pastor. I would have to transition from being the "holy handyman" to the disciple-making pastor. That doesn't seem like a terribly big shift on the surface, but trust me, it is enormous.

It is enormous, first of all, because of the congregation's expectations. Congregations expect that the pastor will take care of all their needs. Church is for the churched. The Great Commission is for the special called missionaries, the ones we raise money for every year at Christmas. That value is deeply imbedded in most congregations in North America.

The church must change its role from being the caretaker of the parish to being a mission outpost.

(2) The focus of ministry must move from the mainstream of society to those in the margins. Once the church begins to realize that the pastor is not the handyman or the caretaker of the parish, they will begin to take care of themselves. They will, with guidance, find ways to do their own pastoral care. Then everyone is liberated to move from maintenance to mission.

Jesus modeled this for us. He reached out to those in the margins—the lepers, the Samaritans, the poor, the adulteresses, the fishermen, the vagabonds, the tax collectors. But he did something else significant. He invested his life in making and equipping disciples who, one day as a result of his tutelage, would turn the world upside down.

It took Jesus three years to instill his model in the lives of the Twelve, many of whom were marginalized themselves. The religious establishment never caught on to this kind of discipleship. But Jesus changed the value so dramatically that a new structure was eventually created—the church. What a magnificent structure it has been!

One should not expect that changing such values is easy. It will take years, but some things can be done in the interim as values are changed in this transitioning process.

At Mission, I preached it regularly. Not every Sunday, lest the congregation overdose on the value or the preacher, but I did give them a regular offering of sermons whose theme was mission over maintenance.

I found another forum that was helpful in changing values. We publish a monthly newsletter. I would write radical articles—usually quoting someone else, of course—and then ask the question: "What do you think?" As time went on I got bolder. Pastor friends of mine who were on our mailing list would call me and say things like, "Boy, you better be getting your résumé updated." By the time I had gotten that bold, most of the congregation was with me. The value had been changed. Again, all of this took time—months, years.

Those in the margins are usually those with addictions in our society. I remember going through one period when it seemed that every new person who came to our church had a drug or alcohol problem. Some were already in twelve-step programs; others needed to be. To me, this was an affirmation that our mission to the marginalized had become effective.

Contrast this to what would have happened several years ago. It would have been difficult for a drug addict or alcoholic to feel a part of our church. All I could hope for was to get them involved in a twelve-step group away from the church. Now most of them at least feel comfortable being "mainstreamed" into the life of the church. They see themselves as fellow strugglers with the person sitting next to them in the pew.

What has made the difference? We have changed a value over the years. Creating a climate of openness and acceptance changed it. The authentic gospel of Jesus Christ reaches out to those in the margins. When this authentic gospel is integrated into the fabric of the church, everyone sees himself or herself as marginal because after all, we are all sinners saved by grace. For some, the sin is drugs or alcohol; for others, it may be a sexual sin or cheating or lying.

When an open, mission-minded church is created, people with little church experience will be attracted to the church. They will not know how to act; they will know little "church etiquette." Their children will not understand what the children of the old congregants know about not running in the sanctuary or wearing their caps during worship. They will not be able to sit still when they're "supposed" to sit still according to the unwritten rules of church culture. The result will be that worship services may have a steady parade of children going in and out at inappropriate times. They are inappropriate from the standpoint of the old church culture, but the new people who come with a hunger and thirst for Jesus will not understand.

All of this will be upsetting to many people, including pastors. I grew up in a church culture when I knew that from 11:30 to 12:00, the time of the sermon, I dared not move or even think about using the bathroom. My dad was a strict disciplinarian who only had to look at me with furrowed eyebrows and I knew what to do or not to do. Contrast that with the MTV children who come to church sometimes with parents (and sometimes without parents) who have little, if any, church background. For one thing, the sermon must be presented in a way that holds their attention at least for a few minutes. For another thing, the congregation needs to be prepared for the disruptive and disorderly behavior they bring to the sanctuary as it moves from reaching those in the mainstream of society to those on the margins.

(3) The congregation must view itself not as parishioners to be served but as missionaries to the local communities. As values begin to change (see points 1 and 2), structures will begin to emerge based on the new values. Parishioners will begin to see themselves as people on a mission. People on a mission are called "missionaries."

In a recent Sunday morning service, I stood at my usual place on the front row. During the praise and worship time of our 8:30 service, someone came up behind me and put his hand on my shoulder and said in my ear, "Could I have a couple of minutes to share something from the Missions Emphasis Group?" "Sure," I replied. I gave Adam the couple of minutes he requested. His plea was for the congregation to bring a pile of clothing the next Sunday "as high as the pastor's head." They had identified families in the community with an immediate need for clothing. Adam and his group saw themselves as missionaries to the community. The next Sunday, I walked out for the 8:30 service to see a huge pile of clothing that, if stacked vertically, would have been as high as my head.

Notice another dynamic that was at work there. My own values had done a 180-degree turn over the years. In the early years of my ministry, I would have been reluctant to allow Adam to speak. I would have been hesitant to trust him to take up some of the valuable "sacred hour." Besides, he should have called a few days earlier, and I could have put him on the program in the bulletin and even coached him about what to say. Adam simply spoke from his heart, made his plea, and sat down—Adam the missionary. The sick and dying institutional church does not allow for spontaneity. Its goal is to control and in the process to suppress the freedom of God's people to fulfill their calling.

How did I come to trust Adam at that point? Before values can be changed, they have to be identified. Several years earlier we had adopted our "core values" as a church. We actually already knew what they were before we voted on them, but Baptist churches have to vote on everything and so we did with our core values.

Once the values are identified, the process of teaching the values to the congregation must take place. Bill Easum and others have called this imbedding the congregation with the church's DNA or genetic code. This begins with new member orientation and then is constantly done through leaflets, Sunday school lessons, small group discussions, sermons, etc. I knew Adam had the genetic code. He understood the mission of the church and his role as a missionary. Trust was not a question. I knew Adam was not a loose cannon.

(4) Discipleship must move away from making good citizens and move toward making disciples. Discipleship. Discipleship. Discipleship. We exist for one reason—to make disciples. Disciples of Jesus Christ are different from good citizens in a number of ways:

- Disciples of Jesus Christ follow only one flag. It is actually a cross.
- Disciples of Jesus Christ are more than good; they *do* good.
- Disciples of Jesus Christ are radical revolutionaries. They stir up the *status quo* in society by being salt and light.
- Disciples of Jesus Christ are the brightest bulbs on the tree, not necessarily in terms of intelligence but where it counts—in allowing the light of Jesus that is in them to shine for the whole world to see.

We Shall Not Be Moved

The power of the old values cannot be underestimated. We sailed along for a couple of years changing this and changing that without much overt opposition. Then the time came to begin a new adult Sunday school unit that we call Adult Bible Fellowships (ABFs).

There was a small vacant room in an upstairs wing of the church. Beside that class was the Fact Finders Class, which consisted on a good Sunday of a group of twelve to fifteen early seniors (fifty to sixty-five-year-olds). We needed the space they occupied in order to knock out a wall and have room for the newer and bigger ABF.

A piece of cake, we all thought. I even volunteered to be the one to make a plea to the class. These were my people, I thought. They were, after all, only slightly older than me. I had played golf with this bunch, ate many fellowship meals with them, blessed their babies and grandbabies—no sweat.

The Sunday morning arrived. I hadn't bothered to call anyone in advance to ask for time on their morning's agenda. It would only take a couple of minutes, I reasoned. They would see the need and gladly move across the hall to a somewhat smaller room that was even decorated a little nicer. I sauntered in and asked the class leader if I could have a couple of minutes to "share something with the group." He graciously submitted.

I made my plea, presenting the case that this move on their part would enable us to reach the "unchurched and unsaved" in our community.

"Thank you," I concluded. "You won't need to make this move for a couple of months, and we'll help you move the chairs and chalkboard when the time comes. Any questions?"

At this point, I fully expected someone to say, "No problem, preacher, we understand the need and we'll be glad to switch rooms." That didn't happen.

The first question was more like a battle cry. "We don't even have enough nursery workers now. Where are all these new people going to put their babies? Somebody was up here just last week begging us to serve in nursery. When we were raising our children, we brought them into preaching with us every Sunday. Why do these young people think they have to have a nursery every Sunday?"

Another battle cry went up. This time the battle lines would be drawn over the furnishings. "We all chipped in and bought these curtains, not to mention the carpet. Now you're asking us to pick up and leave all this behind. Those young couples will ruin this carpet with their coffee and doughnuts."

"I don't think they should be allowed to have refreshments during Sunday school," another chimed in, "We're here to study the Word of God. Let them eat at home like I do."

I tried to get the discussion back to the burning issue of the day, which was reaching the unreached and winning the lost, but my case was hopeless by now. I soon thanked them for their time, asked them to pray about it, and let us know of their decision. I wasn't surprised when one of the class leaders came by my office after Sunday school to inform me that they had discussed it, prayed about it, and voted not to move.

I told the leadership of the new ABF what had happened and admitted my defeat. Someone said, "I think we can out-pray them." The group did move eventually, but it took several months and much weeping and wailing and gnashing of teeth. The start of the new ABF was delayed. During this time, the early seniors were known as the "We Shall Not Be Moved Class." Don't underestimate the power of old values. What were the old values in this case?

- Maintenance over mission
- The church gathered over the church scattered
- Taking care of each other over being on mission
- Being served over serving
- An "our-church" mentality as opposed to a "church-on-mission" mentality

Lo, the Resistance You Have with You Always

There will always be pockets of resistance in the church. Some people will draw a line in the sand and hold out until their last breath. Our "We Shall Not Be Moved" group stood at a distance and watched as the church changed before their eyes. They had not been a part of the new movement of the Spirit. They now would become the last holdouts. Their battle cry was "Remember how great things used to be."

Will there ever come a time when practically everyone is on board with the changing values? Not likely. Resistance persists. Sometimes the opposition is silent and even dormant, but it is always ready to become a voice of opposition. This may sound pessimistic or fatalistic, but I believe resistance to the advancement of God's Kingdom is deeply imbedded in the church. Sometimes it is an underground movement, sometimes it is overt and above ground, but it is always there, always.

Not a Gated Community

It seems that the church always has to fight the battle of exclusivity. Alan Roxborough said the church is "not a community that happens to do mission. It is missional."[2] The church is not a gated community. It is in the world, multiethnic and multicultural. In Romans 6 we learn that the powers of this world have been broken. We are to be different from the world but not living in isolation or in constant battle.

Our tendency to perpetuate the organizations of the church places the church in a maintenance or management mode. It then begins to lose sight of its mission. When things go wrong and the old structures do not work, what do churches usually do? They reorganize with new structures so that the institution can be maintained and perpetuated to the next generation. This is nothing short of being plain wrong. We are not told to go and make institutions but to go and make disciples.

A missional church witnesses to what God is doing in the world. It constantly asks, "What is God doing?"[3] When it discovers what God is doing, it joins him in his work in the world. In 1 Peter 1:1 we read, "To God's elect, strangers in the world, scattered throughout Pontus, Galatia, Cappadocia, Asia and Bithynia." The church is not a "we-shall-not-be-moved" crowd. It is scattered throughout the world and therefore is constantly adjusting its structures and its life to be on mission with God.

I wish I could tell you this is easy. That would be far from the truth. I saw John Maxwell in a video simulcast recently. He spoke about moving from a maintenance church to a mission church. First of all, he made it clear that "You have to work real hard." That needs to be heard loud and clear by anyone with the fortitude to try to change values in a church. A few sermons, no matter how fantastic, will not do it.

Then Maxwell had this advice in the form of four questions:[4]

- Can I (we) relate effectively to the "influencers" in the congregation?
- What is the mission of the church? Can the leaders and the congregation articulate the church's mission?
- Do the "influencers" buy into the mission? Can I (we) get them to own it?
- Will the "influencers" help pass on the mission of the congregation?

Legitimizers

Bill Easum said we don't just count our opposition; we weigh it. Maxwell's "influencers" become critical at the point of changing values. I prefer to call them legitimizers. Legitimizers are people in the congregation who carry a lot of weight in terms of influence, respect, and admiration. They are the leaders whether or not they have a leadership position. One such legitimizer for me was Don. Don was as solid as a rock. He would often take me aside and tell me that what I was doing was right but that I needed to go a little slower. He served in various leadership roles in the church. Watching him was like watching a master artisan. I learned a lot from Don about the importance of legitimizers. They must be sold on the church's mission or everybody is in for trouble. Count yourself blessed indeed if the legitimizers catch the biblical vision for the church early. If they do not, be careful about moving forward until they do.

Get off on the wrong foot with enough legitimizers and you might as well pack it in. This is where some of the hard work of transitioning comes in. You must devote time to get the legitimizers on board with the church's vision and mission.

Some of the old-timers who have established themselves as legitimizers over the years should not be viewed as the enemies of progress. They do have wisdom to offer. They, in the words of Martin Luther King Jr., "may not get there with you," but they can give their blessing to others who want to birth something new. Don't hesitate to ask them for this blessing. They deserve the respect of being asked for it, and you will need it before going forward.

I remember asking that question to a senior citizens group at a critical point in our transitioning. I acknowledged that they would likely have trouble accepting some of the new ways. I made an unabashed appeal for their input, their resources, their time, and their prayers. But then I asked them for their blessing. Some gave it immediately; others took more time. Make no mistake—that blessing is important.

Affirm The Pioneer Spirit

It is also helpful to appeal to the pioneer spirit in people. A few years ago, someone gave me a photograph that now sits on a table in my office. It depicts a lone snow sledder being pulled behind a team of dogs across a frozen tundra. The caption reads, "Do not follow where the path may lead, go instead where there is no path and leave a trail."

Americans have the pioneer spirit. So should followers of Jesus Christ. Jesus was a pioneer. He carried people in their thinking to places they had never been before. So did Paul. Paul took the cross of Christ across the continents, blazing new trails with the gospel. He set up outposts all across the Roman Empire in places like Ephesus, Corinth, Colossae, Derbe, and even Rome itself.

We were pioneers indeed. We had submitted ourselves to the Potter and he was molding us into something new, a new receptacle for his Spirit. Lewis and Clark were such great heroes in American history because they were pioneers.

When people in the church step out on faith, they need to be publicly affirmed and their pioneer spirit celebrated. We adopted change as one of our core values. Change agents are pioneers. When they launch out with bold new initiatives in God's kingdom, they need to be recognized and affirmed. I have kept a quote from Helen Keller (source unknown) in a file for years. It reads, "Life is either a daring adventure or nothing. Security does not exist in nature, nor do the children of men as a whole experience it. Avoiding danger is no safer in the long run than exposure."

The Church Constitution

Finally, what about the church constitution? Some churches don't even have them. Constitutions are more important in some denominations than others, usually depending on church governance. I tend to agree with the school of thought that says, "Don't ever look at it. Then you can plead ignorance when you violate it."
Church constitutions have usually been created and amended *ad infinitum* for one reason—to keep somebody in their institutional place. We have learned in most cases that it is far, far better to ask for forgiveness than to ask for permission. This is not to advocate being deceitful or dishonest. I am simply advocating that we move forward, with the utmost integrity, to carry out the Great Commission.

The mission statement of Willow Creek Community says that their mission is to "turn irreligious people into fully devoted followers of Jesus Christ." Ours is not stated as such but in essence it is "to turn religious church members into fully devoted followers of Jesus Christ." That is no small task. It is a God-sized assignment. I believe that Willow Creek's mission is a piece of cake compared to churches like ours.

One of the perils of writing this story in book form is that someone somewhere will get the idea that what we have done can be duplicated simply by following a few principles. True, transitioning is and must be principle-driven. But it is first and foremost Jesus-driven. One's values can only be changed through a life-changing experience with the Christ who could not be contained in a tomb and who certainly cannot be boxed into a few neat guidelines for religious reform. Don't look for a "Transitioning Kit" coming soon to your nearest Christian bookstore.

Ready for Radical Reform

By 1994 we had begun to change values in rather significant ways. Disciple-making became a rallying cry if not a stated core value. God began his work of renewal and people responded. Holy discontent had been created and dealt with in essential ways. Early in 1994 we signed on to participate in something called T-Net, an intentional disciple-making process founded by Bob Gilliam and Bill Hull. It required a leadership team to travel to Atlanta, some six hours away, for a total of six Saturdays over two years.

T-Net necessitated a major overhaul of our structures, including the way we did Sunday school, missions, evangelism, worship, and Bible study. We joined about fifteen churches from all over the Southeast in the process. By the end of the two years, our church was the only church who had come anywhere near completing the process. Why? Because we had already begun to change our values several years earlier. It is absolutely essential to change values before changing structures.

John Bunting is the head football coach at the University of North Carolina. In a November 14, 2001, interview posted on www.goheels.com, Bunting talked about what he described as the "culture of Carolina football." The storied history of Carolina basketball has overshadowed what happens on autumn Saturdays on the gridiron. Bunting understands the daunting task that lies before him: that of changing the image of the school to a football school. He talked about the laidback attitude of the fans who habitually arrive late to the stadium on Saturdays, preferring to socialize in the parking lots and downtown watering holes rather than arrive early to their seats. He also understands that in order to change what happens on the football field and subsequently on the scoreboard, he must change the culture and values of the whole program. Football is more than just X's and O's (structures). It is also about values – it is about creating an atmosphere and climate that perpetuates passion and vision.

What is true on the collegiate football fields of our land is equally true in the churches of our land. In order to change structures, we must first change values. It is a constant battle for the loyalties of the congregation. It is a battle that begins in the hearts and souls of each member of the congregation.

Dying to Self

In order to change, one must first die to self. It is in dying that we live. That is central to the Christian message. When we die to self, something new is born in us. When we have been changed from the inside out as individuals and churches, the structures will fall into place. They can be borrowed from mega churches, meta churches, microcosmic churches; it doesn't matter. The structure isn't the thing. The transformation of values paves the way for even old bones to live again.

Notes

[1] Quoted by Eddie Hammett in *The Gathered and Scattered Church* (Macon GA: Smyth & Helwys, 1999), 76-77; Mike Regele, "Renewing the Church for the 21st Century," address presented at Northern Baptist Theological Seminary, Chicago IL, 8 November 1998.

[2] Alan Roxborough, speaking at the "Leadership Institute" of the Cooperative Baptist Fellowship, 27 June 2000.

[3] Ibid.

[4] John Maxwell, simulcast seen at the Hollifield Learning Century of the Baptist State Convention of North Carolina, 18 October 2000.

The Laws of Wingwalking

Several years ago I did an internet serach on "wingwalking" and found a wonderful website that highlighted a wingwalker named Lisa Perdue. She danced on the wing of Walt Pierce's 450 Stearman, *Ol' Smokey*. Lisa flew with Walt at air shows across most of America. Below are excerpts from her book, *Let's Take a Wingwalk*.

Each maneuver was explained to me in detail, as though I was retaining the information. I familiarized myself with the wingstand, its locks on the straps that would hold me in place, and was instructed on where to stand to avoid crashing through the wing's fabric.

We flew once around "the patch," a take-off and landing, perhaps three minutes in the air. Mostly this flight was to determine how my neck would tolerate the pressure of the wind. Then there was the nagging question of whether or not to trust that harness enough to be tipped upside down in it 700 feet over a concrete runway. I decided the harness could be tighter.

For all my lack of breath, still I slipped in that harness going inverted. After a few rapid heartbeats I realized that dousing my waist in oil wouldn't get my hips through it and began to relax. About then is when my goggles flew off my face but were caught by a loop attached to the back of my helmet. My hands would not go in the direction I aimed them, nor would the goggles have been there to greet them if they had. Both were wildly sporadic in the wind. I absolutely was not ready to let go of the stand at this stage of my career, my eyes hurt, and this "____ Big Harley" was upside down and very, very loud. Wear earplugs. But more importantly, I realized this . . . the wing is no place to panic. Everything is more easily grasped when one is calm.

Rules for Wingwalking

- If you do, use a biplane.
- If you have a biplane, make certain your pilot is capable of flying a person on the wing.
- Prepare yourself. Your next fifty wingwalks will not be like the first. You will not likely "get used to it."
- Wear earplugs, suitable clothing, goggles, and a helmet.
- Do not practice in weather below 75 degrees.
- Do not expect to get rich.
- Do expect constant and multiple bruises and to be pelted with bugs.
- Realize that you are about to do something almost no one else wants to do—and for good reason.
- Change your mind.

Let's adapt these rules for wingwalking to transitioning a church.

Rules for Wingwalking and Transitioning a Church

(1) If you do, use the right equipment. Metaphors are an important tool for doing church in the twenty-first century. The airplane is fine, but I prefer to use the metaphor of a ship or train. They don't have wings, but biplanes don't have enough passenger seats to make the metaphor work.

(2) Once you've properly been equipped, make sure your pilot (pastoral staff and other church leaders) is qualified to get you (the church) where you want to go. The pilot doesn't have to know everything but should have some knowledge of how to navigate and use the rudder. At least the pilot needs to know how to get the thing off the ground.

(3) Be prepared. There will be contingencies. Every day in the transitioning process will be different. There are no maps. No one has filed a flight plan for you. You are pretty much on your own. There are a few essential principles you can follow, but you must rely only on the wind (the Spirit) for guidance. You will not get used to the turbulence and the bugs hitting your goggles. You will need to be mentally tough.

(4) Wear earplugs and a thick skin. This attire will insure that you will not be distracted by the noise. Transitioning is noisy. You will also face cold and sometimes harsh winds. Goggles and a thick outer garment will be a necessity or you will be battered by the winds of resistance.

(5) Check the temperature. If the climate isn't right in the church for change, then forget it. You will put your life in serious jeopardy. You can begin to work to create a climate for change, but you must understand that church climatic conditions don't change overnight the way the weather does.

(6) Do it for the right reasons. You probably learned a long time ago that you aren't going to get rich in the ministry, at least not financially. Transitioning a church should be done only when you sense a divine purpose in it all. If you operate from the motives of self-aggrandizement, vengeance, or pride, then forget it. The experience is harrowing enough when operating from pure motives.

(7) Do expect constant and multiple bruises and to be pelted with bugs. I know, this is verbatim for wingwalking on an airplane, but there doesn't seem to be any way to improve the wording. Bruises will come. The Apostle Paul experienced beatings. You may not get this physically, but I can guarantee that there will be Monday mornings when you will be battered beyond recognition. The bugs—well, they will come at you from all angles. Goggles and other proper clothing will help (refer to 4). What are some of the bugs? Let me name a few: your motives will be questioned, you will be accused of not being a good pastor, you will be ostracized by your colleagues in the ministry, you will be alienated by your best friends. Bugs hitting your face at 200 miles per hour can be messy. The impact stings beyond anything you can possibly imagine.

(8) Realize that you are about to do something almost no one else wants to do—and for good reason. Wingwalking is risky business. This is why many seminarians are looking at becoming church planters, i.e., starting new churches, rather than immersing themselves into a stagnant and traditional situation. Most people prefer to remain safely on the ground. Some

even come out for an air show and strain their necks looking upward at the fool on the wings. Most pastors and other church leaders would rather remain snuggly fitted into the old paradigm, the one that remains firmly anchored on the ground. It is comfortable there and warm, and there are certainly fewer bugs with which to contend.

(9) Change your mind? Do it before you get airborne and certainly before you get out there on those wings. Once you're off the ground, you're committed. To abandon the mission in mid-flight is certain disaster. You must be in it for the long haul. This isn't a program from your denominational publishing house that you can guide the church through in thirteen weeks.

(10) Don't let go of one thing until you have a firm grip on something else. This isn't one of Lisa Pardue's laws, but she did imply it: "I absolutely was not ready to let go of the stand at this stage of my career, my eyes hurt, and this '_____ Big Harley' was upside down and very, very loud. Wear earplugs. But more importantly, I realized this . . . the wing is no place to panic. Everything is more easily grasped when one is calm."

I submit to you that this should be the first law of wingwalking for anyone brave (and foolish) enough to transition a church: Don't let go of one thing until you have a firm grip on something else.

How This Works in Church

Let's look at practical applications of these laws of wingwalking. First of all, the leader who would become involved in transitioning should ask hard questions:

- Is the change really necessary for Kingdom purposes?
- What do we hope to accomplish by instituting the changes?
- Is the change worth the hassle?
- What kind of change are we talking about?
- When will the change take place?
- What will be accomplished when the change takes place or what will the church look like once the change is implemented?

• Is most of the church on board with the vision for change? Remember, sometimes it is more important to weigh the opposition than to count it.

Once these and other pertinent questions have been answered, it is time to proceed. Remember that abrupt change almost always upsets. This is where preparation comes in. No one in their right mind would try wingwalking without a great deal of preparation and practice and without getting key personnel in place.

This first law of wingwalking—Don't let go of one thing until you have a firm grip on something else—is in stark contrast to the practice of many clergy. I have noticed this especially among young wing-walkers. Fresh out of seminary or Bible college, they are ready to take on the world. Their style is more suited to the military than church leadership.

Many of them practice the "see-a-hill-take-a-hill" mentality. This may be a daring military strategy, but it is not recommended for churches. The scorched earth policy also works well for military operations. General Sherman is still talked about in the South for practicing this strategy. In this strategy, the marching army burns everything in its path before moving on to the next town or village. The reason is clear: leave no supplies or resources for the conquered foe to rebuild and retaliate.

Such strategies are for war. True, we in the church are engaged in spiritual warfare, but that's supposed to be with the world and the forces of darkness, not with each other. Spiritual warfare does take place inside the church, but our primary battle is with the forces of darkness on the outside.

Applied to Sunday School

Early in our transitioning we felt it necessary to radically change the way we did Sunday school. T-Net taught us that we needed open groups if we were going to be effective in doing outreach and evangelism.

We had two choices: transition existing adult Sunday school classes into the Adult Bible Fellowship (ABF)[1] concept, or create a new unit implementing the ABF principles from the outset. We chose the latter.

Concurrent with this strategy was the dual strategy of transitioning an existing class that was already using some of the principles but lacked intentionality and structure. The new ABF began to grow rapidly. They were quick to adopt the four-pronged purpose of ABFs: outreach-evangelism, fellowship, Bible teaching, and assimilation.

One of the goals from the beginning was to create at least one new ABF every year. We began this strategy in 1996 and by mid-2001, we had begun five new units using the ABF principles. The old class that we began to transition is still at about the same place it was five years ago. They are reluctant to organize along the ABF model, they have not grown by any appreciable numbers, and they constantly battle stagnation and lack of vision.

Meanwhile, we have left alone three other adult classes. We have suggested some things from time to time along the ABF model, but have not insisted that they transition.

I can only imagine what would have happened in our setting if we had adopted a different strategy. What would have happened if we had tried to tell all the adult Sunday school classes that they had to cease and desist what they were doing and begin promptly to operate out of a new paradigm? I am certain that the outcome would have been disastrous. That kind of scorched-earth policy would probably have been the demise of my career and the church would have become embattled and embittered.

By beginning these parallel structures, we were practicing the first law of wingwalking: Don't let go of one thing until you have a firm grip on something else. We held on to the old way of doing Sunday school while at the same time we grabbed a new way. As of this writing, we are still in transition. I don't anticipate that we will completely let go of the old model until a few more years pass. But we are going full speed ahead in creating new ABFs, and from these ABFs, numerical growth has come in our church.

This is not a sales pitch for doing Sunday school in any particular way. ABFs work for us. Something else may work better in other settings. I am advocating that we follow the first law and principle of wingwalking: don't let go of one thing until you have a firm grip on something else.

Applied to Worship

We have applied the same principle in other areas of church life. In 1996 we began to talk about our desire and need to adopt a more contemporary style of worship. The old hymns, organ music, and choir anthems were not doing it for many people. We also discovered that a contemporary Christian radio station was becoming popular in our area.

Our ministers of music at Mission Baptist Church, Kolis Moore and Koni Huneycutt, have been wonderful as "outside-the-box" thinkers. We knew that percussions (drums) would make a lot of traditional worship people nervous. Thus, instead of abandoning the traditional service, we chose to begin a new worship service using contemporary music and a more sensory-oriented style. It has worked with phenomenal success. Now, almost five years later, we have begun to transition the traditional service because the numbers dwindled rapidly.

This new style of worship wasn't popular with the whole congregation in the beginning. After a couple of years, however, the doubters were seeing so many new people come to Christ that they were sold that maybe we were doing the right thing. Some of them still aren't ready to embrace the new style, but at least they give their blessing to it.

A middle-aged couple came to the new service for the first time about three years after we had started. The man grew up in the community and was fairly well known by local people. After a few minutes into the service, a couple of people heard his wife say to him, "He's here." "Who's here?" the husband asked. "Jesus, Jesus is here." When word of that conversation spread to a few of the traditionalists, they became more convinced that perhaps this new style of worship had merit after all.

Applied to Small Groups

The same strategy has worked at least in one other important area in the church. T-net taught us that it is important for a church to have closed groups as well as open groups. Modeled after Jesus and the Twelve, small, closed groups provide an intimate setting where in-depth Bible study and accountability can occur. Again, the principle was the same as with worship and Sunday school. We created a parallel structure that enabled us to birth something new while at the same time maintaining the old.

It wasn't that the old wasn't working for a number of people. It continues to work for them. Why destroy something that is working?

Our first small group met for nearly a year as a parallel structure in the church. Fourteen people, including myself, made up this accountability group. We used workbooks as guides for studying the Bible and growing as disciples. After a year, we had equipped others within the group to become small group facilitators. We also kept reminding them throughout the year that while they were growing by leaps and bounds in their faith, they were never to view themselves as spiritual elitists. An elitist attitude damages the body of Christ. This happens frequently in churches where Bible study groups take on this kind of attitude. Resentment grows and the transitioning process is thwarted if not totally derailed.

The Early Church

At the same time, old paradigms that continue to work for some will not work for others. The book of Acts teaches us that the early church did not abandon temple worship right away. The Gospels show that it was the practice of Jesus to be in the synagogue on the Sabbath. In Acts 3:1 we are told that Peter was going up to the temple at the time of prayer when he encountered the crippled man. This was after the Upper Room experience, after Pentecost. Were these early disciples practicing the first law of wingwalking? It would appear so. They were holding on to the old; i.e., temple worship (after all, they were still Jewish) while at the same time moving forward to usher in the age of Christianity. Eventually they would abandon parts of their Jewish heritage, especially when it conflicted with their new understanding of God as revealed in Jesus Christ.

Bill Easum says that people who didn't grow up in church have an enormous advantage in their Christian walk than those who did. He feels this way for two reasons: They don't have as much to unlearn and they will better understand the meaning of Incarnation.[2]

Those who have little or no church background will be able to do wingwalking better than those who grow up in the church. They will be more enthusiastic about grabbing hold of something new, and they will not be as reluctant to let go of something old. When a church begins to transition, it will likely have more people who grew up in church than those who didn't. As the transition begins and continues, there will be more and more people in the church who do not have to overcome this handicap. The problem with the church's leadership is in working with both. Wingwalking is scary for anyone. Put a bunch of nervous and scared people together, and you have a recipe for conflict.

Wing-walkers are risk takers. Not everyone likes to take risks and not everyone likes risk takers. Many will stand on the ground and watch as spectators but will not dare take the chance to get out on the wing themselves. Moreover, although they may not admit it, they find a small amount of glee when wingwalkers fail and tumble to the earth.

Wingwalking Begins on the Ground

It will help to understand that wingwalking actually begins before the first step is taken outside the plane. I would suggest that the following be applied before undertaking the rather risky adventure of wingwalking:

- Pray for courage while still on the ground.
- Get the plane airborne; wingwalking isn't impressive on the ground.
- Trust the pilot. You can't walk on wings or water or anything else without him.
- Get out of the plane. It is much safer inside the plane and you will be tempted to abandon the notion of wingwalking in favor of the comparative comfort of the plane.

Don't Tear Down that Fence

John Maxwell has good advice at this point.[3] He says a common statement of resistance is this: "You're leaving behind my traditions and what I value." His answer? Don't leave them all behind. In fact, Maxwell asserts, "You need to know why a fence was put up before you tear it down."

In Barbara Kingsley's *The Poisonwood Bible*, the fundamentalist missionary in the novel insists on the practice of baptism by immersion for the Congolese villagers. Their refusal to be baptized infuriates the hardened preacher. It was years before he realized that their refusal to be baptized had nothing to do with their resistance to the gospel. It had to do with the fact that the villagers still remembered with great horror the day one of the village girls was devoured by an alligator at the same spot in the river where the stubborn missionary insisted they be baptized.

Sacred cows may be sacred for no other reason than the simple fact that someone's revered grandmother donated them. Trust me, that's a fence you had better not try to tear down.

All of this is about balancing the constant tension between knowing what to change and what to leave alone. There are paradoxes to balance. Travis Collins identified some of them.[4]

- *The need for things to change and yet to stay the same.* Change is imperative if the church is to survive and be effective in the twenty-first century. Paradoxical to the need for change is the unchanging nature of Jesus Christ, "the same yesterday, today, and forever." In a chaotic world, people have the need for an anchor. It becomes necessary then to provide some sense of continuity with the past and with the "rock of ages" while simultaneously changing to remain ahead of the world.

- *The fear of being too forceful or too foolish.* One of the risks is the danger of losing all credibility by appearing to battle windmills. It is important to balance these two paradoxes in order to avoid the perception of being downright foolish.

- *The need to study and the need to honor interruptions.* Much of Jesus' ministry was done through interruptions. While on his way to one place, the blind and the lame came to him for healing. Sometimes even his disciples were frustrated by the constant interruptions and tried to send people away. While Jesus always took time for these people, he also understood the need to withdraw from the demands of working miracles. He withdrew frequently to pray and be with God. It is fair to say that Jesus was transitioning an entire religious movement, but in that process he saw the need of withdrawing from the distractions of this world. Here is where we have to do a real balancing act. We will operate at less than maximum efficiency if we do not spend a great deal of time in study, meditation, and prayer.

- *The question of when to let go.* Clergy and other church leadership do not have to be control freaks to feel apprehension about letting go. Sometimes it is easier to go ahead and do the work rather than wait for others to discover, develop, and deploy their spiritual gifts. It is important to resist that temptation.

- *The need for passion and the need for moderation.* Simon Peter seemed to have struggled with this paradox. His impetuous nature compelled him to plunge ahead with great passion. As time went on, he learned to balance these compulsive passions with moderation. Remember the *chaordic* concept. Plunging ahead with nothing but passion sometimes produces an unproductive chaos. This must be coupled with order and organization.

Let Go Anyway!

All this talk about not letting go of one thing until we have a firm grip on something else can begin to sound like playing it safe and avoiding taking risks. Nothing could be farther from the truth. Wingwalking is a risk, no matter what precautions we take. Wingwalking is never equated with playing it safe. Another point is that sometimes we have to let go even when there is nothing else in sight to grasp.

Eugene Peterson makes the point that "creation, true creation, is always unprecedented and unmanageable." It is adopting a "There-was-never-anything-like-this before" mentality.[5] Taking risks, however, is not the same as being reckless. "But the moment tidiness and conduct become the dominant values, creativity is, if not abolished, at least severely inhibited."[6]

A wing-walker cannot possibly eliminate all risks. Nor would he or she want to do so. To eliminate all risks is to stay on the ground. Even with all the preparation and safety precautions, and even when there is something in sight to grasp, there comes a time when the wing-walker must let go of the old and grasp the new reality.

This is called trust in the Holy Spirit. This trust even goes beyond seeing a new and safe reality to hold on to. Sometimes it means letting go when there is nothing in sight but a promise and a prayer. Take these risks with forewarning. Make sure the Holy Spirit is the one calling you to let go. Other forces will lure you to do so, but listen only to the Spirit of God. Wing-walkers should follow no other spirit but the Holy Spirit—not the spirit of intuition, not the spirit of instinct, and not even a gut feeling.

Notes

[1] See Knute Larson, *Growing Adults on Sunday Morning* (Wheaton IL: Victor Books, 1991).

[2] Bill Easum, *Leadership on the Other Side* (Nashville: Abingdon, 2000), 16.

[3] John Maxwell, simulcast at Hollifield Learning Center of the Baptist State Convention of North Carolina, Hickory NC, 18 October 2000.

[4] Travis Collins, "The Paradoxcial Tensions of Leading," *Current Thoughts and Trends* (September 2001), 16.

[5] Eugene Peterson, *Under the Unpredictable Plant* (Grand Rapids MI: William B. Eerdmans, 1992), 164.

[6] Ibid., 165.

Morphing

meta-mor-'pho-sis—change of physical form, structure, or substance esp. by supernatural means.

I will constantly morph maverick methods if that is what it takes to win a few. (paraphrase of 1 Cor 9:19-23)

Chapter 7 was about changing values. This chapter is about change *as* a value. A couple of years ago we adopted our "core values" as a church. One of them is change. It reads, *As Christians we cannot accomplish God's will by staying the same. We live in a rapidly changing world; and, therefore, we must change in the way we do ministry in order to remain relevant. However, we affirm the timeless and unchanging nature of the gospel message.*

God, in his infinite power and knowledge, is able to change the course of human history in the twinkling of an eye. It usually takes God's people a lot longer than that. It only took a few days for the Hebrews to get out of Egypt. The plagues, the breaking down of the pharaoh's will, the threat of continued destruction, all eventually resulted in the release of the Hebrews. Remember, however, that they weren't released into the promised land. They were released into the desert.

The question of how long it took the Hebrews to get out of Egypt is moot. The key question now becomes *How long did it take to get Egypt out of the Hebrews?* Let's start with forty years. That's the length of their desert wandering. Even then they weren't fully ready to conquer and inhabit

Canaan. It was another pagan world like Egypt. It would take several more generations to get paganism out of the Hebrews.

Insert Change and Stand Back!

Brian is a friend of mine who pastors a large downtown church in a major city in North Carolina. He shared with me one day about how he, the staff, and lay leadership had felt the need for change in their church for some time. The church is a typical downtown church—institutional, high-maintenance, old school. They were in slow but steady decline for about three decades. The problem was that the congregation was in denial about the decline, as is often the case.

Brian and his leadership team decided that they needed a contemporary worship service. They spent time studying some of the models already in place.

After careful study, they eventually decided to go with an 8:30 Sunday morning format. It would be followed by Sunday school and then the more traditional worship service at 11:00. By using contemporary music, they hoped to attract young families who were church dropouts or who had never dropped in.

The 8:30 service succeeded in attracting new people. Conversions resulted from the service. In a couple of years, leadership was emerging from the early service. Within three years, the church was experiencing no small amount of turmoil and Brian, his staff, and lay leadership had a new problem—how to deal with the turmoil without ripping the church apart.

As Brian shared his story, it was obvious that he spoke through a lot of pain brought on by the turmoil. Brian also issued a warning for all of us that needs to be heard loudly and clearly: when change is introduced into a system, it has a ripple effect throughout the whole system. How true this is for a church!

Many churches have jumped on the contemporary service bandwagon (no pun intended). "Contemporary" usually means the introduction of a praise band replete with drums, guitars, keyboards, and the like. The music is usually much more upbeat and louder than usual in church. This has proved to be upsetting to many old paradigm people in churches, especially the part about the music being louder.

Change as a Value

Changing values before changing structures does help with the transition immensely, but change can still have far-reaching impact that no one can anticipate. It is essential, therefore, to adopt change as a value. There must be room for constant morphing.

Bridges are built with change in mind. Years ago, engineers learned that concrete, steel, and other building materials expand when subjected to heat from the sun and warm weather. The change is not much, only a few inches across the span of a river. But without "expansion joints," those few inches of expansion cause the bridge to crack, buckle, and eventually become unsafe.

"Expansion joints" must be built into the fiber of the church. When even the smallest change is implemented, it will affect the whole church in dramatic ways. "Expansion joints" are needed to absorb some of the change.

The Church Building

Let's use the "expansion joint" metaphor for the church building itself. Effective churches in our day need to adopt a less static view of church buildings. Buildings have become part of the institution. They have become symbolic of all the maintenance that has to be done to the institutional church. Buildings must be maintained. Transitioning a church from a program-based church to a ministry-based church may require that the church change its attitude toward buildings.

Thomas Bandy is the senior editor of *Net Results*. In addition, he is the author of several books on churches in transition and a partner in Easum, Bandy, & Associates, one of the premier church consultant teams in North America. In a recent article, he wrote these words of wisdom:

> If the small church wants to thrive in the new millennium, the members have to see their building for what it is: a tactic. It's a tool, a method, one vehicle among many to motivate and launch Christian people into mission. Rip out the walls, remove the pews, unscrew the hardwood . . . in heaven's name, load that thing on a flatbed truck and move it 500 yards down to the paved

highway where the mini-mart and the people are. Do whatever it takes to make that building a tool for God's mission.[2]

Now imagine bringing that as a proposal to the next church business meeting. Yet, that kind of attitude must be adopted if churches are to be effective in the next few decades. In what kind of church would this take place?

• a church that has adopted change as a value
• a church that is not married to the institution
• a church that has visionary leadership
• a church that has moved from a maintenance to a mission mode
• a church that is willing to morph anything and everything for the sake of the gospel

William Willimon said that the role of the clergy is to keep the community (church) nervous about who they are.[3] This is part of the prophetic role that the pastor must play from time to time. However, as already noted (see chapter 6), the pastor who tries to do this abruptly and without compassion will find himself or herself at the end of the unemployment line fairly quickly.

Change Must Begin with the Clergy

Change as a value needs to start with the clergy. I think it has become a core value in my personal life because I have been consistent in doing the following things:

• Read everything I can get my hands on about change. Recently I have even delved into the nonreligious realm with books like *Who Moved My Cheese* by Spencer Johnson and Kenneth H. Blanchard, Dee Hock's *Birth of the Chaordic Age, Good to Great,* and *Built to Last: Why Some Companies Make the Leap…and Others Don't* by Jim Collins. I would also recommend several journals such as *Net Results, Rev., Leadership Journal, and Faithworks,* among others.

- Join with other clergy and church leaders who are on the cutting edge of change. I currently participate in two groups. One of them is a local clergy group that I took the initiative to convene. We read books together and meet over lunch weekly to discuss the chapter we've read. The other group is a "learning community" group pulled together from across my state. We only meet every few weeks and we meet about the issue of "Transitioning Churches."

- Pray. This is a given and should go without saying, but I think it needs to be said anyway. Sometimes we forget that no real church reform or spiritual revival has ever been achieved without being bathed in much prayer.

- Practice mentoring. I have found it helpful to be both on the receiving and giving end of mentoring. The benefits of having a mentor are obvious. A mentor can give support, provide accountability, and help one stay sharp. Being a mentor can also be helpful. *Iron sharpens iron* is the way Isaiah put it. An emerging concept in the corporate and church world is the coaching concept. Coaching brings together the best of mentoring, equipping, discipling, and encouraging.

"Chaordic"

We've already mentioned how messy change can be in a transitioning. Dee Hock, founder and former CEO of Visa International, has coined the phrase "chaordic." It is a combination of the words *chaos* and *order*. When the credit card was distributed to the masses in the late sixties, there was the potential for chaos. Hock realized that this chaos theory would be tested in a serious way. The system eventually worked well because every branch manager of every branch bank in the United States and eventually throughout the world was imbedded with the values of the parent company, yet they had to be given the autonomy to act on their own. Out of this chaos came order. Thus the term "chaordic."

That is the perfect term to describe the church. In the modern age it was desirable and even relatively easy to control and measure the programs and growth of the church. Except for a few Pentecostal spasms here and there, the church looked like a well-run Madison Avenue entity. That may have worked to some degree in a churched culture. Now, with the vast majority of the culture unchurched, something more is needed.

Let the church return to chaos! Out of chaos, God created the entire universe. God's creation cannot be controlled or measured. The church ruled by the Holy Spirit will be a messy, chaotic church. Things will seem out of control at times. Control freaks will not be comfortable in the church of the postmodern age.

That doesn't mean, however, that God isn't in control or that things are completely disordered. The order comes when all the disciples (church people) are imbedded with God's genetic code of spiritual disciplines, Christian practices, or whatever you prefer to call them. Therein lies the order. But don't look for order in the way the church is organized to carry out its mission. If order is ever restored, the mission is in danger of being lost.

When people are desperately hungry, it is difficult for them to line up in neat formations and wait to be fed. They care little about how things look. They want to be fed. Similarly, when people are spiritually hungry, their desperation will cause them to seek spiritual food and meaning without thought to how things look on the surface. What matters is that they are spiritually fed. "If the church takes advantage of the spiritual hunger in today's society, it will be able to minister more effectively than it has in centuries."[4]

Centralized vs. Decentralized

I had a long conversation with an old paradigm pastor a couple of years ago about whether the church should be centralized or decentralized. He argued for a centralized, hierarchal structure with the final authority resting with the pastor. In his model, if a church member wanted to begin a ministry, they would have to go through a chain of command to get everything approved. It's no wonder little creative ministry happens in this kind of closed church system. One gets tired of jumping through hoops.

In a decentralized system, there is little, if any, church hierarchy. One can begin a ministry one day and tell the church about it the next day. The pastor and staff are available as resources and even consultants, but neither the staff nor the lay leadership must give approval for every action.

This "chaordic" model involves trust and empowerment. It also assumes that the church members are growing disciples. Growing disciples are being imbedded with the values and beliefs of the church (the genetic code) and can indeed be trusted to do ministry.

There is a church in another part of my state that is a good example of the centralized system. A few years ago the three staff members—senior pastor, associate, and youth minister, all ordained—happened to be out of town at the same time. There was a death in the church family and none of the staff could come immediately to the home of the deceased. This presented a crisis for the congregation. They began to ask questions about why none of the paid staff members were at the office. A committee brought a recommendation to the church in a business session that at least one of the ordained staff members had to be in the office at all times, 9-5 daily. The proposal passed overwhelmingly.

That kind of closed and centralized church system makes a false and absurd assumption that only the ordained clergy are empowered to do real ministry. In an open, decentralized system, the following would have happened:

- The ordained clergy would be expected to be out of the office as much as possible, out in the real world equipping the disciples of Jesus known as church members to do the ministry.
- Any number of church members could be called on to minister to the bereaved family.
- The gifts of all disciples would be recognized and validated, not only those of the professional clergy.

The development of this kind of paradigm doesn't happen overnight. Old habits are difficult to break. Old dependencies are hard to overcome.

A Continuous Process

Morphing is a continuous process. Transitioning never ends. The steady mantra must be sounded over and over. Does there come a time when the church can relax and say, "Well, we have morphed. There's no turning back now. The change is so entrenched that we would never go back to the way it was before"? I don't know the answer to that question, and furthermore I am afraid to find out. I do not want to find out. I do know that I would die a spiritual death if I had to go back to the old paradigm.

Church leaders involved in transitioning must understand that the process is never-ending. Many begin the process and then become so overwhelmed that they give up. This is one of the major causes of what is generally called "clergy burnout." It is difficult, it seems, for clergy to accept the fact that there often is no "end game" with transitioning. Moses never saw the promised land. It must have been difficult for him to devote his whole life to bringing a people through the desert and then not go there with them.

Transitioning is always open-ended. There is no closure, no moment when we can rest and say we have done it. It is a continuous process. Rewards are great for the church that transitions, but if the church leader is looking for a neatly-wrapped package with finishing touches, he or she will be greatly disappointed.

Brian McLaren of Cedar Ridge Community Church near Washington, DC, has said that there are two things church leaders need to do:

> First, come to grips with the epochal change as our culture transitions from a modern world to a postmodern world. Second, we have to come to terms with the fact that we live in a post-Christian culture. This means we have to approach our culture with a missionary strategy as though we were presenting the gospel for the first time. Christian faith thrives in this kind of situation and provides us with wonderful ministry opportunities.[5]

Study the first-century church as we find it in the books of Acts and the New Testament epistles, and you will find a church in a constant state of metamorphosis. This is the nature of the church. We'd do well to get used to it.

My learning community for transitioning pastors reflected at the beginning of 2001. Here is a list of what we had learned:

- Act decisively and quickly in some situations, but not all. Pray for wisdom to know the difference.
- Find ways to unleash creativity in the church.
- Build and utilize corporate wisdom to plan and manage change and transition.
- Move with the "remnant" who see the new and don't let the naysayers hold you back.
- Conflict is inevitable in change.
- Choose the battles you will fight.
- When you begin change, there are always ripple effects.
- Create or find a place to share the pain you experience as a leader during the process of transitioning.
- Watch and plan for generational reactions, and note that the mind-set of individuals or groups is often more a key element than generational issues.
- "Tossing grenades" into certain areas of church life is often necessary to find and deal with issues that have been hidden or not discussed for decades.
- Reinventing self and staff creates fears and is tough, but it is worth it.
- Church and business deal with change in different ways. Businesses makes decisions fairly decisively; churches have to process.
- There is a holy discontent in the church that often initiates change.
- There are times when the pastor must move from being a priest to a prophet.
- There is a deep loneliness among those in the "holy discontent" category.
- We often measure the wrong things in church life, and therefore new standards of success and effectiveness must emerge and be integrated into decision-making and budgeting.

Now, I implore you, does any of that sound like a neat process where there is a definite starting point and a clear ending point? I don't think so. Did seminary prepare us for any of that? Not likely. Is this going to be messy? You bet!

We Are Drifters

There is a ton of evidence in the Bible that God's people, if left to drift and wander, will turn away from God. Hosea lamented this. Hosea 11 is a sad chapter in the Bible and in the history of Israel. God reminds his people of all he has done for them. He has birthed them, taught them to walk, brought them out of slavery. Yet they still turn away from him. God is saddened by their failing commitment, but he doesn't give up on them.

Return, O Israel, to the LORD your God. You sins have been your down-fall! Take words with you and return to the LORD. I will heal their waywardness. We will never again say "Our gods" to what our own hands have made, for in you the fatherless find compassion. (Hosea 14:1-2, 4 NIV)

If left to ourselves, I am afraid that we will slip back into whatever is most comfortable to the gods of our own making. The church of Jesus Christ should never be comfortable. Now, more than a decade after Mission Baptist began to transition, the steady drumbeat of change continues. We use articles in newsletters, sermons, private conversations, constant prayer—whatever it takes. Continuous vigilance is needed to shake people out of their comfort zones. The pastor or church leader who thinks he/she can get to a point where everything is fixed and there's nothing else left to change is in for a rude awakening.

It is important that no sacred cows be allowed to take life. In the words of Winston Churchill, *never, never, never, never, never give in.*[6]

God modeled something important for us in the way he dealt with Israel. He refused to give up on them. In the same way, we cannot give up on transforming and reforming the church.

Can a church live again? I agree with Findley Edge at this point: "I believe the church can be renewed because it provides us with the greatest reservoir of people committed to God that can be found anywhere."[7] I am similarly optimistic. In fact, there is strong evidence that the church is being renewed. A new reformation may actually be in the embryonic stages. Many churches are dying and many more will die. Some will go gracefully and peacefully. Others will die a slow, agonizing death. Some are killing themselves. They are like nicotine or drug addicts who can't seem to stop their destructive behavior. However, I believe that God, in his sovereignty, is allowing this to happen so he can birth something new.

God is constantly renewing: "The old has passed away, the new has come" (1 Cor 5:17).

Job, devastated by disease and disaster, asked the question of the ages: "If a man dies, will he live again?" (Job 14:14 NIV). We may well ask the same thing of the church: If a church dies, will it live again? The answer, I believe, is a resounding yes. It may not survive in its present form, but it will survive. I also believe that we are living in some of the most exciting days of the church's 2,000-year history. There are signs of renewal all around. Some have likened our day to the first century, and we read in church history what an exciting time that was. It was also a dangerous time, a time fraught with risks, but it was exciting.

A couple in our church, Bob and Jane, teach a Sunday school class of young adults, roughly ages eighteen to twenty-five. Just getting such a group together on Sunday morning is a huge challenge. Some days the room is full, on other Sundays Bob and Jane may be the only ones. They have shared their frustration with me on more than one occasion. I helped them pray for excitement, for signs of life to become evident in the class. A young man named Travis began to show up regularly. Travis was different from the other class members. He sought spiritual guidance because his life had become a wreck at the age of twenty-one. He had been involved with drugs and other dangerous behavior. Frankly, he was an ill fit in the class. After a few weeks, he invited a couple of his friends. These "three amigos," as I call them, brought new life and excitement to the class—probably more than Bob and Jane had bargained for. Their lifestyles and language were radically different from those of the existing class members, most of whom grew up in church and never strayed far from it. It was almost as if the "old-timers" in the class resented newcomers coming in and asking crude questions and making unorthodox statements. These "old-timers" were in their early twenties.

We had prided ourselves in being what we thought was an "open" church. By that I mean a church that is open to newcomers of all kinds of backgrounds. We learned quickly that "morphing" is a constant process. We can never grow comfortable and complacent in our holy huddles.

What challenges do we continue to face as we morph toward an authentic body of Christ? We are only beginning to see new vistas and visions that God is opening for us.

(1) Become a safe and helping place for addicts. I believe it is true that addictions of all kinds are the new dimension of sin in the twenty-first century. We have made progress in accepting the addict, but much more is needed. The reality is that most people in recovery still don't fit in at our church or anybody else's. Ministries like Celebrate Recovery started by Saddleback Community Church in San Diego have had success in helping recovering addicts find hope and help in the local church.

(2) Help people find a way to grow spiritually when their lives are so full they hardly have time to breathe. Spiritual formation and discipleship "on the fly" will continue to be one of our greatest challenges. People have time, of course, to do almost anything they want to do. The problem is that new Christians lack the spiritual maturity to understand the importance of spiritual formation, and they don't give it priority. One of our greatest challenges in this "time-poor" world is to find a way to help young adults grow spiritually to the point that discipleship is a top priority in their lives.

(3) Continue to shift discipleship from taking everyone through an identical process of groups and workbooks to the dynamic experience of uniquely and personally customizing a process for every individual. I'm not sure what this will look like yet. The process is apt to be messy and complex, but it will become essential to have a customized approach to making disciples. The post-modern era is producing a culture that needs relationships more than certificates.

(4) Continue to grow toward becoming an open church that accepts people where they are. We have made progress in that area, but as evidenced by the experience of the "three amigos" mentioned previously, we still have a long way to go.

(5) Be willing to make hard decisions in the future that will move us forward. The temptation and tendency is to rest on our laurels and believe the lie that we have already transitioned, that we have somehow arrived at our destination. Morphing is a continuous process. As of this writing, we face major decisions about starting a third worship service. The challenge is

finding a time slot and space. We may have to move off campus to do so. The other alternative is to provide the worship service at a time on Sunday morning that will raise huge staffing issues for Sunday school and scheduling. We may have to consider finding other ways besides Sunday school to help people grow spiritually and find help in discovering and carrying our their God-given mission.

(6) Live with a holy expectation that God is going to do something beyond human ability. Ephesians 3:20 speaks of God "who is able to do immeasurably more than we can ask or imagine." Once we start to box God in a formula or process, we begin to limit his capacity to work in us. Do we live with the kind of holy expectation Paul talked about—that God is going to do the unexpected?

These particular challenges and others may be unique to our particular situation. However, the point is that every church will face new challenges as it continues in the transitioning journey.

A pastor in another part of my state came up to me recently at a conference we both attended. He wanted to know if I thought transitioning a church was worth it. I knew what he was talking about, considering the high cost transitioning can exact on a church and a pastor's life. I thought for only a moment before I replied that yes, I thought it was worth it, at least for the scores of people now in our church whose broken lives had been mended, whose despair had turned to hope, and all those who had once given up on the church but now found it to be a vital, life-giving entity in their lives. I thought of Donna Gabbert (see chapter 2) and others like her who might not have found Christ if we hadn't done the hard work of transitioning.

Is it worth it? Every person and every church will have to answer that for themselves. I don't believe I would have the energy to do it again in another church. It is a lifetime endeavor. My friend who wanted to know if it was worth it went on to make a valid point. Most often, he argued, it is far easier to begin a new work than to attempt a transition of an existing church. The traditions and the traditionalists who keep them are simply too rooted in their ways, and in some cases it is not even possible.

Job asked the question, "If a man dies, will he live again?" The title of this book is derived from that verse by simply substituting one word to read, "If a church dies, will it live again?" Can a church live again? That is ultimately left to God in his sovereignty, but I can only respond the way Job responded in the same verse: "All the days of my hard service I will wait for my renewal to come."

Notes

[1] Scripture paraphrase by Ron Martoris in "Kaleidoscopic Leadership," *Rev* (March/April 2001), 74.

[2] Thomas Bandy, *Net Results* (September 2000), 10.

[3] William Willimon, *The Last Word* (Nashville TN: Abingdon, 2000), 136.

[4] Barry Winders, *Net Results* (July/August 2001), 3

[5] Brian McLaren, quoted in *Current Thoughts and Trends* (September 2001), 3.

[6] Stephen Mansfield, *Never Give In: The Extraordinary Character of Winston Churchill* (Nashville: Cumberland House, 1995), 142.

[7] Findley Edge, *The Greening of the Church* (Waco TX: Word Books, 1971), 16.

Epilogue:
What I've Been Thinking Lately

Most of the time we operate on automatic pilot when it comes to our opinions and ideas. We cruise along assuming that what we've always thought is the way it should be. The church in transition can never operate on automatic pilot. A consistent "no fear" attitude is needed. I recently took a week off for a personal retreat in the mountains of southwestern Virginia. During that week I read and thought and prayed a lot. Such times are necessary for the leadership of a transitioning church. Such times also lead me to mediate and contemplate, which helps me rethink things. Here are some of the questions I tossed around that week and since:

• What if we completely revised the whole idea of what church is? What if we began to create a church that was not for the benefit of its members, but instead we began to equip ourselves for the benefit of the world?

• What if we devoted most of our church's resources—buildings, budgets, staff, etc., not to the healthy but to the sick? In other words, we determined that our mission is to the irreligious, not the religious.

• What if the goal of our ministries and programs is not to get people to come to church but to get people to carry out the mission of the church in the world?

• What if we sent spiritual growth groups (adult Sunday school classes, small groups, etc.) out to study movies, concerts, sports events, shopping malls, bars, video game parlors, campgrounds, synagogues, and mosques? Then we could come back and open and study God's Word and talk about what we've seen, what's going on, and what it means to be a Christian in our world according to the biblical revelation.

- What if we not only tried to add one new Adult Bible Fellowship (adult Sunday school class) every year, but we also tried to add a new worship service every year or two designed to reach a different segment of the population that we are not currently reaching—Gen Xers, different ethnic groups, grandparents, just to name a few?

- What if we began something like a ministry village on our grounds with buildings to house ministries to unwed mothers, homeless, job services for the unemployed, marriage counseling, career counseling, language and job skills for Hispanics, and countless other ministries?

- What if we helped close to 100 percent of our regular attenders discover their spiritual gifts and then helped each of them use their gifts for the expansion of the Kingdom of God?

- What if we began something called "community ministries" in which we had a full-time staff person to help coordinate the church's involvement in community organizations like schools, clubs, recreational organizations, nursing homes, and others?

- What if we challenged everybody in the church to be involved in at least one mission experience every year? These "mission experiences" would include everything from overseas trips to one-day projects down the street. They would include a time of coming together for prayer, Bible study, and other preparations for the participants. Then after the project was complete, there would be a time of more prayer, Bible study, and debriefing as the group came together again for reflection. Actually I issued this challenge to our church in a sermon dated June 29, 2003, that by the beginning of 2006 everyone in the church would be involved in such a mission experience. Stay tuned.

It is not enough to ask if a church can live again. That is a no-brainer, considering that God is able to raise the dead and birth the new. The church that would continue to live and remain a dynamic force for God in the world will, I believe, have to continue to ask: What is God doing next?